HOW TO MA
CHOO
YOU

GW00818890

HOW TO MAKE THEM CHOOSE YOU

YOU

Derrick Scott-Job

SOUVENIR PRESS

First published 1994 by
Souvenir Press Ltd
43 Great Russell Street, London WC1B 3PA
and simultaneously in Canada

ISBN 0 285 63202 7 casebound
ISBN 0 285 63186 1 paperback

Photoset by Rowland Phototypesetting Ltd,
Bury St Edmunds, Suffolk

Printed in Great Britain by
The Guernsey Press Co. Ltd, Guernsey, Channel Islands

Contents

PART THREE: CULMINATION

Preface

Redundant—what a depressing word that is. If you are reading this book because you have been made redundant you are probably feeling insulted, unwanted, a drop-out, guilty of having failed yourself and your family, and you'll be downright depressed.

On the other hand, you may be reading it because you simply want to change your job without there being any pressure on you to do so. You, of course, have a head-start on your fellow readers who are redundant because you have the advantage of job-hunting from the comparative strength of having a job rather than the much more unenviable state of being out of work. But your objectives are the same—to find a new job. You are both embarking on what may be a long campaign to achieve what you want, for which you have to get into training and develop a strong sense of self-discipline and determination. So bear with me while I have a word with your redundant colleagues, then we can all move forward together.

To most of us redundancy means 'surplus to requirements, no longer wanted, superfluous'. My dictionary agrees, but if I read on to an alternative meaning it says: 'deprived of one's job because *it* is no longer necessary.' *It* is no longer necessary, not *you* are no longer necessary. This is a very important distinction, and one which you must take on board and accept before you can begin to compete in the job market with your more fortunate rivals who are changing their jobs voluntarily.

Yes, *rivals*! Every applicant for the job you want is a rival with whom you are just as much in competition as you would be if you were running a marathon. You have got a great deal of hard training ahead if you are going to win, which you surely can.

The problem is that, although you all have a common objective, your starting points are different and no two of you will have identical circumstances.

You will shortly be meeting John Taylor who has been made redundant, and he will tell you how he felt and how he started to think positively. John Taylor is lucky in that he is happily married and has a very supportive family who will do all they can to help him through the traumatic period between being made redundant and finding another job. Unfortunately, not everybody is as lucky as John. *You* may not be.

So you will also meet Chris White who is divorced and lives alone in a rented flat. His problems are very real indeed, not only emotionally but financially. You may relate to John or to Chris or, more likely, be somewhere in between.

Then again, you may relate to neither John nor Chris but to Sally Fraser, a 28-year-old research assistant with a medium-sized advertising agency which has run into financial difficulties. You will meet her, too.

Of course, you won't match any one of these three characters in every detail, but near enough to enable you to adapt their circumstances to yours and give you a realistic starting point. You will soon discover that the method by which you are going to achieve your objective will be the same, whoever you are. You will have the same preparation to do for your job-getting campaign; the same financial problems to cope with, although your solutions may well be different; the same need for a well-prepared and presented CV; and the same need to develop your skills at responding to interviewers.

Don't expect miracles. Reading this book will not *guarantee* that you will get a job—in the end that will be up to you. But it will ensure that you avoid many of the pitfalls which will inevitably eliminate you when it comes to the crunch and it will greatly increase your chance of success. Let's move on, then, and meet John, Chris and Sally.

Meet John, Chris and Sally

JOHN TAYLOR

On the day it all started, John Taylor returned to his office after his lunch break at 1.30 p.m.

It was Thursday, 11th August (the day after his 40th birthday). There was a note on his desk saying that his Director, Arthur Williams, wanted to see him and would he please go to his office some time after his return from lunch.

A polite note, thought John. Usually when his boss wanted to see him it was a curt message to come to his office immediately. John had a busy afternoon ahead so he decided he had better go and see the old man now and find out what he wanted. Straightening his tie, he left his office and walked briskly down the corridor.

'Come in,' called Mr Williams when John knocked on his door.

'You sent for me, Mr Williams?'

'Yes, John, I did. Come and sit down. John, we've been very pleased with the way you've been running your department recently, which makes my job this afternoon even more difficult.'

'Is there a problem, then?'

'Yes, John, I'm afraid there is. As you know, sales have been taking a hammering over the past few months and things are not looking any easier in the immediate future. As a result the Board has decided it's got to make some economies, and unfortunately your department is the one that's going to suffer . . .'

John realised that he was gripping the arms of his chair as though the dentist's drill had got past the fillings and was now drilling out the nerve. Mr Williams was still droning on. John tried hard to concentrate on what he was saying.

'. . . we're going to combine your buying department with David Henshaw's . . . Now, as you know, David is senior to you, but nowhere near retiring age, so he'll take over the new combined department and we've no option but to make you redundant . . . You've no idea how sorry I am about this.'

John could not take in what his boss was saying. Why was he sorry? Mr Williams was pleased with his work—he said so. Yet he was sacking him. He must have misunderstood. He couldn't be sure whether he'd passed out or was just about to.

Somewhere in the distance he heard his voice say:

'Mr Williams, are you telling me I'm sacked?'

'Yes, John, that's what it comes to if you put it bluntly.'

'I don't know what to say . . . If you're pleased with my work, couldn't you transfer me to somewhere else in the company?'

'John, if I could I would, believe me. But we've got to save costs if the company is to survive, and the only way to do that is to reduce our staff. You're one of the unlucky ones. I know it won't help you, but you're just one of fifty people I've got to give the same message to this afternoon.'

'So what happens now?' John asked.

'I suggest you take the rest of the afternoon off. Go home now and break the bad news to your wife, then tomorrow you can talk to Dick Makin in Personnel, who'll go into all the details of redundancy money with you—I really am sorry, John.'

John walked back to his office in a daze. The truth still hadn't sunk in. I'm out of a job . . . Why me? I never dreamed anything like this could happen to me . . . What did old Williams say? Take the afternoon off and break the bad news to Sheila . . . how on earth am I going to do that? And what about the children?

To hell with his busy afternoon! To hell with the company—to hell with everybody. He grabbed his briefcase and left, slamming the office door behind him.

*   *   *

John Taylor had left school at 16 and, because of his passion for cars, had managed to get himself a job at the Oxford Motor Company.

After serving his apprenticeship he had been promoted from the shop-floor to management and had been put in charge of a small department responsible for buying many of the electrical components and accessories used in car manufacture. He enjoyed his job and now, at the age of 40, had thought he would spend the rest of his working life with the company.

His wife, Sheila, had worked as a secretary until their marriage twenty years ago, since when she had taken on the traditional role of looking after their children and their home. They had a son, Richard, aged 18, who had just started working, and a daughter, Sarah, aged 16, who was still at school and hoped to go on to college and train as a veterinary surgeon.

They lived in a comfortable semi-detached house, just outside Oxford.

All in all, the Taylor family was just what a lot of other families would like to be—content, happy together, no debts to speak of, and a rosy family future ahead of them.

Then it happened—that fateful afternoon when he was made redundant . . . and, despite a generous redundancy cheque for £20,000, the outlook was far from rosy.

CHRIS WHITE

Chris had been another apprentice who had joined the Oxford Motor Company at the same time as John Taylor and after his initial training had become a skilled toolmaker. He had been appointed section leader in the tool shop and then transferred to Training where he had been put in charge of training new apprentices in toolmaking. He would have been in line for a management job, but it did not work out that way.

As part of the cutback by the company in all its departments, it changed its policy regarding apprentices and stopped taking them on. With no apprentices to train Chris was truly without a job and he, like John, was made redundant.

Although he had served the company for the same length of time as John, he was on a lower salary and his redundancy package was £10,000—half the sum which John received. But his real problems were domestic. He was divorced and lived alone in a rented flat. He was paying £800 per month maintenance to his wife who had custody of their two children. He had no capital except for his redundancy money and, of course, no income other than the dole.

Apart from his financial worries he found it very hard to overcome his depression and the feeling of loneliness when he got up in the morning without a job to go to or anyone to talk to. He was in danger of very quickly spiralling downwards and blowing his redundancy money in the local pub.

SALLY FRASER

Sally was in her late twenties when she lost her job as a research assistant in a medium-sized advertising agency, which was going through a rough time, having lost two of its largest clients.

Her home was in Cheshire and she shared a London flat with a girlfriend. Her regret was that she had not gone on to college for further education and had no special training or qualifications. After leaving school she had got a job as a cashier in a local supermarket. Several jobs had followed, including clerical work with a chain of bookshops and a publisher. Her next job had been as a receptionist with an advertising agency where she also helped with media research. Finally she had moved to another advertising agency as a research assistant, and this was where she was working when she was made redundant.

She had been with the firm for five years, so she was entitled to the full statutory redundancy payment, but this only amounted to about £1,000 and the firm, which was in serious financial difficulties, could not afford to top this up with an ex-gratia payment.

Nevertheless, Sally was a resourceful girl. After the initial shock she very quickly pulled herself together and began to make plans. Soon she was ready to think about coping with her problems and finding out how she could begin a new career.

*   *   *

How to get the best value from this book—whether you are a John, a Chris or a Sally—is explained in the next section.

About This Book

This book has been developed from real-life experience after studying the strengths and weaknesses of a large cross-section of people when they are communicating with each other—and good communication is the essence of successful job-getting.

It goes right back to basics. Some people might criticise it for being too basic and even call it patronising. Well, I make no apologies for that. Most people think they are pretty good at communicating, just as most motorists think they are the perfect driver when they get behind the wheel of a car. But when they find themselves competing with several hundred others for the job they really want, they discover that perhaps there are shortcomings in their approach which they never thought of as weaknesses. So keep an open mind and bear with the advice which may sometimes seem trivial and unnecessary to you.

A word or two, now, about the contents of the book and how you can get the maximum benefit from it.

It is divided into three parts: the first is called PREPARATION; the second, ACTION; and the third, CULMINATION.

PART ONE: PREPARATION

Before you start applying for interviews you have a lot of preparatory work to do. You will need a CV, for instance, but
you have a long way to go before you can start preparing it.

When you have lost your job, for whatever reason, you
are in a state of trauma, so your first step is an emotional
one which you have got to overcome. Everybody deals with
this problem differently, and we shall examine some of the
remedies at the beginning of Chapter 1.

Financial problems loom large when you are first
unemployed and in Chapter 2, which I have called 'Your
Business Plan', you will find advice on preparing your budget
and then, equally important, a method of monitoring it during
the year so that you are not faced with unexpected and unwel-
come surprises.

Working from home often presents special difficulties if you
have not been used to it. How to cope with the problems
without disrupting the rest of the household is dealt with in
Chapter 3.

If you have not been made redundant but are simply planning to look for a better job, you may think that these first
three chapters have no relevance for you. Certainly you will
have no emotional hurdle to cross before you can start planning, but you will have other difficulties—not least the fact
that you are working in a full-time job and cannot give your
whole attention to your job-hunting campaign.

You should bear in mind that you will have to budget for
additional expenses, and you will also need to devote part of
your free time, in the evenings and at weekends, to working.

So do at least read Chapters 2 and 3, for they will help you
to organise yourself much more efficiently before you begin to
follow the advice in the rest of the book.

Whether you are still employed or not, you need to know
how the job market works—how vacancies are filled—and this
is the subject of Chapter 4. Then follows the all-important

chapter on how to get into training to become a 'professional' interviewee. Once you have accepted the need to get into training and started to implement it you are well on the way to getting interviews and performing well in them, which will greatly increase your chances of success.

You will then be ready to prepare your CV, but first you will have to research your past history very thoroughly to discover the Real You. You will need to recall every detail of your education and your past job experience. And you will need to make a personal assessment of your own strengths and weaknesses, so that whatever the interviewer asks you about your past experience, you can answer truthfully and without hesitation. After completing your own personal assessment in Chapter 6, you will find that there is much more to the Real You than you realised. There is so much that you take for granted and would not think of telling an interviewer. This chapter will tell you how to capitalise on your strengths and how to cope with your weaknesses.

There is a great deal of conflicting advice written about the content and the production of a CV, and I shall discuss the pros and cons in detail in Chapter 7. It is, without doubt, 'the most important document you will ever write in your life', because your future livelihood will depend on your getting it right. You will need to take time over it.

The production of your CV completes Part One of the book and of your preparation. You will now be ready for action and to start your campaign for getting interviews.

Failure to get interviews is generally due to lack of proper preparation, so I cannot overstress the importance of preparing thoroughly *before* you start applying for interviews. Failure at interview is also nearly always due to lack of preparation. So be patient and get your act together before starting Part Two and launching yourself on to the job market.

PART TWO: ACTION

You now have one objective—to get interviews. Succeed in getting the interviews and, when you have learnt how to handle them properly, the job offers should follow.

What is sometimes called the 'normal' way of getting interviews is to reply to job advertisements in the press; there are other ways which I shall deal with later on. Where to look and what to look for are the subjects of Chapter 9.

It will also be helpful for you to know what happens to your letter of application when it reaches the company, because this will influence both the content and its layout. So, in Chapter 10 we shall visit the personnel department of a typical company and find out what action they take when a vacancy arises and how the applications are dealt with.

Reading an advertisement is not enough. You must read between the lines to find out what the advertiser is really looking for. Analysing an advertisement in this way will help you to write a more appropriate letter of application and, therefore, stand a better chance of being called for an interview. I shall deal with this analysis in Chapter 11.

The letter of application is the key to securing an interview. Whilst you may well have only one CV for all occasions, your letter of application will be tailored to match what you believe the company is looking for as a result of your analysis of the advertisement. Each letter will be different, but each will conform to certain rules which will be explained in Chapter 12.

Finally, this part of the book will identify self-marketing techniques and opportunities for job-hunting other than the traditional method of reading the job vacancy advertisements, such as using the services of an agency and round-robins.

PART THREE: CULMINATION

The third part of this book concentrates on your performance at interview—selling yourself to the interviewer by highlighting your strengths and successes and demonstrating how you can meet the company's needs and contribute to its prosperity.

As any good salesman knows, in addition to demonstrating the selling points of his product he must also assess his customer so that he knows how to approach him. You must do the same with the interviewer and this is discussed in Chapter 15.

Chapter 16 explains how to perform well at interview and includes examples of a poor performance and a good one. You will have the opportunity of appraising the poor performance before studying how it should have been done.

Sometimes there will be more than one interview. The objective of the interviewer at the first interview is to *eliminate* unsuitable applicants and so draw up a shortlist for the final interview which will be conducted by the *decision-maker* who can say 'yes'. Your approach to the two interviews will be different and I shall explain the reasons why in Chapter 17.

All that remains is the contract of employment, the most important aspects of which are included in Chapter 18.

*   *   *

To get the best from this book you must work through it at a sensible pace and make sure you understand and accept the advice given in each chapter before you go on to the next one. You will gain nothing by hurrying it.

Many of the chapters involve written work (such as writing your CV, analysing an advertisement and writing letters of application), but others contain a great deal of detailed information and present a number of ideas, some of which may be new to you. At the end of these chapters you will find a series of questions which you may care to answer and which will help to ensure that you have a thorough understanding of the points which have been made. Model answers to the questions appear at the end of the book. The alternative is for you to read through the chapter again before continuing.

Move on now to PART ONE for the first step in preparing for your campaign.

PART ONE
PREPARATION

1   First Steps

'I was absolutely shattered. It was all so sudden. My sacking was totally unexpected—I had been with the company for 23 years and it never occurred to me that I wouldn't always be with it.'

That was John Taylor's first reaction when he was told that he had been made redundant.

'Next morning I went to see Dick Makin and he went through all the rigmarole of the legal aspect of being made redundant. The only small crumb of comfort was that the company was going to make a generous redundancy payment of £20,000, although by law they were only obliged to pay me a little over £5,000. A lump sum of £20,000 sounded all right. At least I wouldn't have to start collecting the dole money—not yet anyway.

'The worst part was telling the family. I really felt I'd let them down, even though it wasn't my fault.

'As far as I was concerned I was finished. Who was going to employ me at the age of 40, especially with my limited experience? I'd only ever worked for one employer. I felt as though I was at the bottom of a well with the whole world looking down on me—sniggering.

'I collected my £20,000 redundancy cheque and said goodbye to the Oxford Motor Company for the last time.

'I'd never had £20,000 in the bank before. It was as though I'd won the football pools, and since I truly believed nobody would ever employ me again, all I could think of was that we should pay off the mortgage and then Sheila and I should take the biggest and best holiday we'd ever had. Probably the last we ever would have! Richard was 18 and Sarah was 16, so they could look after themselves while we were away. What we would do when we returned didn't seem to matter much.'

John's reaction was typical and perfectly understandable. But he was wrong on four counts. Of course he must sign on for the dole immediately—never mind the £20,000 in the bank. From this moment on every penny counts, because he has no idea how long it will be before he gets another job.

He should certainly not feel that he has let his family down—and neither should they.

He was wrong, too, to think that he was finished and that nobody would ever employ him again. All the doom and gloom spread about in the newspapers about being 'too old at 40' and '40-year olds cast on the scrap-heap' is just not true. Thousands and thousands of people aged 40 and over are re-employed even when unemployment is high, *provided they believe in themselves and learn how to attack the job market*. It is only true if you believe it to be true.

He certainly shouldn't use his redundancy money to pay off the mortgage and blow the rest on a holiday. More about that in Chapter 2 when we study how to prepare a business plan.

Of course it didn't happen that way. Fortunately for John he had a level-headed wife with whom he could discuss the problems and who persuaded him to have a cooling off period for a few days.

The following weekend they got together as a family to discuss what to do. Richard had already got a job with a company in Oxford and Sarah was still at school studying for her

A-levels. They took their father's redundancy in their stride and wanted to know when he was going to do the same! Their reaction was the best therapy that John could have had and he had little option but to pull himself together and think about the future.

The first and most immediate task was to work out a budget and make sure they had control of their finances. We shall hear more about how they did this and how they developed their business plan in the next chapter.

*   *   *

John was lucky to have such a stable background and supportive family to help haul him up from the bottom of the well where he found himself after the initial shock of being made redundant.

Chris, on the other hand, was in a far worse plight. Apart from living alone, he is the phlegmatic type, inclined to withdraw into himself and finding any kind of setback hard to cope with. Not only that: his redundancy cheque was half that of John's and even when he was working he had been finding that the monthly payments to his former wife were stretching his resources to the limit. His emotional problems and financial outlook were bleak.

That £10,000 redundancy cheque seemed a lot of money and, like John, his first thoughts were to escape, regardless of the consequences.

Whatever advice he is given, he is likely to ignore it for the first few days and will probably spend more time than is good for him in his local club or pub, just to have someone to talk to. This is no bad thing—provided it is only for the first few days.

His first step to recovery will be when he signs on at the Job Centre as unemployed. This is obviously a practical step to take because it will immediately provide him with an income, however small. But more important, 'signing on' will have an immediate sobering effect on Chris and make him realise that he has got to take some positive action if he is going to make a new life for himself.

At the same time as signing on he will ask about income support and what help he can get with the payment of his rent and the maintenance payments to his former wife.

Whatever support he gets, it is quite obvious even before he works out a budget that he will need some part-time work while he looks for a permanent job.

So, his first priority should be to look for a part-time job through the Job Centre, by scanning the advertisements in the local paper, and by asking everybody he knows for help. Apart from providing a much needed income, there is a lot to be said for being employed, even in only a dead-end job, when it comes to applying for a new job. Any potential employer worth his salt will approve of the initiative of someone like Chris who has made an effort and not just sat around all day with a chip on his shoulder.

*   *   *

Sally was probably more traumatised than either John or Chris when the London advertising agency where she had worked for five years sacked most of its staff overnight to save itself from going bust. At least she received the statutory redundancy pay to which she was entitled and which amounted to just under £1,000.

She had worked in the research department of the agency. She had no special skills, not even typing, but she was a good administrator.

Her first panic reaction was that she would have to give up the flat she shared and return home to Cheshire. Panic decisions are seldom the right ones: her flatmate persuaded her to wait a few days before making any rash decisions and, instead, to use the time to sign on for unemployment pay and find out what additional help, if any, she could get from Social Security.

Like Chris, she should also make it her first priority to find a part-time job by calling on as many agencies as she can. Not every temporary job requires typing or word-processing skills.

*   *   *

There is nothing to be ashamed of in feeling intense shock, self-pity and panic when faced with what appears to be the hopeless situation of unemployment. Those of you who show your emotions and appear to 'go to pieces' are probably the lucky ones, because you will get it out of your system more quickly than the stiff upper lip, stolid ones amongst you.

By all means let yourself go for a few days and, as soon as you can, sign on for unemployment benefit. This will bring you down to earth and will help you get to grips with your campaign for finding a new permanent job. The next step is to prepare your business plan: how you do this is described in the next chapter.

2   Your Business Plan

Preparing a business plan should be your first task.

Why a business plan when you are unemployed? Because you are, in effect, running your own business with one product to sell—YOU. You may be lucky and get a quick sale, but it could take you up to a year to achieve it.

If you are out of a job and have no income you will be living on capital which will eventually run out, so you have got to plan your finances very carefully. If you are a family person this is the time for frank talking with all the family. Whoever can contribute to the family budget should do so. If you were previously the sole breadwinner, this may mean your partner taking a part-time or even a full-time job, for instance. And that, in turn, may mean your sharing the household chores with your partner and fitting these into your work programme without detracting from your main task of finding the permanent job you want.

If you have children of wage-earning age, they too must contribute to the family budget, probably to a larger extent than they have done in the past when you were working.

Getting you earning again is a team effort in which every member of your family must be involved.

If you have no family to contribute to your budget or to

support you, planning your finances is even more important because you will have no one to fall back on if things go wrong for you.

So your first step is to prepare a budget for the next twelve months. We shall study the budgets prepared by John, Chris and Sally. Clearly, your own particular circumstances will not be matched in every detail by any one of the three budgets illustrated, but they will provide you with a check-list to help you work out your own budget. It should also be appreciated that the illustrations were prepared in 1993 and reflected average incomes and benefits at that time. Interest rates, unemployment benefits (to be known as the job seekers' allowance in 1996) and other allowances can change at any time, so you will have to check the current rates when you prepare your own budget.

JOHN TAYLOR'S BUDGET

John Taylor's budget appears on page 33.

The top line shows that he had a bank balance of £1,000 before he was made redundant, which, together with his redundancy cheque, gives a total capital of £21,000.

The first decision that has had to be made is what to do with the lump sum redundancy payment. Some people may decide to set up their own business or buy into a franchise of which there are many on offer. This course of action needs very careful consideration indeed, and is certainly not one to be taken without a great deal of professional advice.

John's wife, Sheila, had been a secretary until she gave up work when the children arrived. The question now is whether she should try and get a job, full-time or even part-time, or whether they should invest part of the redundancy money in a personal computer and printer with which she can offer secretarial services to local businesses from home.

The advantages and the pitfalls of being your own boss are

BUDGET—JOHN TAYLOR

Cash in bank	£1,000
Redundancy cheque	£20,000
Total capital	£21,000
Invested	£20,000
Cash reserve	£1,000

CASH DUE IN

Investment (say 8%)	£1,600(a)
Unemployment benefit	£2,300(a)
Part-time employment	–
Dependant allowance	£350(c)
Wife's income	£7,200(b)
Son's contribution	£750(a)
Total cash due in	£12,200

CASH DUE OUT

Mortgage	£1,500
Council tax	£900
Heat and light	£1,250
Telephone	£500
Food	£4,000
Clothes and cleaning	£500
House insurance	£300
Contents insurance	£150
Life assurance	£1,200
Motor expenses/travel	£1,000
Entertainment	£750
Holidays	£0
Daughter's expenses	£500
Typewriter/files, etc.	£100
Printing	£100
Stationery	£100
Postage	£180
Contingencies:	
Repairs and renewals	£500
Sundries	£500
Total cash due out	£14,030

CASH DUE IN *less* CASH DUE OUT

Shortfall	(£1,830)

(a) 12 months   (b) 9 months   (c) 3 months

outside the scope of this book, but in the Taylor family common sense has prevailed and the need to conserve their capital for an unknown period until John is working again seems the sensible course to take. Sheila has agreed to look for a job and, if she fails, to reconsider working from home later on. In the meantime it is agreed that they should buy a reconditioned electronic typewriter which John will need for his job-hunting campaign. He has never done much typing but is willing to learn.

Richard, who is still living at home, has been contributing £10 per week towards his keep. He has said he could increase his contribution by another £5 if it would help. It certainly would. Sarah has offered to give up her studies for her A-levels and leave school early to earn some money. That has been turned down because it seems that by careful planning they can manage for the next twelve months at least, by which time there is a good chance of John being employed again.

It has been decided to invest the £20,000 redundancy cheque. They have chosen to divide it between two building societies for a risk-free investment in long-term savings accounts, because these will yield the highest interest and they will not need immediate access to the money.

So, they can expect income from the following sources: their investment; John's unemployment benefit; a dependant allowance for Sheila until she starts working in say, three months' time; Sheila's income (for nine months in the first year); and the contribution from Richard. This adds up to £12,200. They will not be liable for tax because more than half of this sum will come from Sheila's earnings and she will be taxed separately.

The Taylors then go through their expenditure, item by item.

They have no outstanding debts except the mortgage which has some five years to run and is costing about £125 per month. They have two cars—a family car which John had used for going to work each day and a runabout which Sheila used for the school run when the children were younger.

Office equipment, printing, stationery and postage will become clear after you have read the next chapter, which describes what you will need for your job-getting campaign.

Even if you are in a similar situation to John, your income and expenditure may be quite different. You may not have a mortgage, for instance, or your expenditure on heat and light may be different depending on the kind of house you live in and whether you have two teenage children living at home. But the example shown is intended to indicate the sort of expenses you may need to consider when compiling your own budget, entering the figures of income and expenditure which apply to you.

Subtracting the expenditure from the anticipated income shows a shortfall of £1,830 in John's budget.

When he first produced his budget there was a shortfall in the year of £2,450. After going through the expenditure again and by diligent pruning this was reduced to the figure shown of £1,830.

The question, then, is how they should finance the shortfall.

They have various options. They could go through the expenses again and prune them here and there, but this would be unlikely to save the sum they are looking for. They could use part of the redundancy money, but this would reduce their income from their investment. The £1,000 cash reserve would be insufficient to fund the shortfall and, in any event, they should have some cash available for emergencies. Finally, they could dispose of their second car, which should more than cover the expected shortfall. They decided that this is the prudent course to take.

The crisis point will arise for the family in three months' time if Sheila fails to get a job and John is still unemployed. If that happens they will have to look at their budget again and rethink their situation and their style of living.

It is not enough simply to prepare a budget.

Expenditure varies from month to month. In John's case, for instance, he pays his heating, lighting and telephone bills

JOHN TAYLOR'S CASH FLOW FORECAST (months 1 to 6)

Budget		Month 1	Month 2	Month 3	Month 4	Month 5	Month 6
£1,000	Cash in hand	£1,000	£332	(£86)	(£1,134)	(£872)	(£620)
CASH DUE IN							
£1,600	Investment income	£133	£133	£133	£133	£133	£133
£2,300	Unemployment benefit	£192	£192	£192	£192	£192	£192
£350	Dependant allowance	£120	£120	£120			
£7,200	Sheila (net)				£800	£800	£800
£750	Richard	£63	£63	£63	£63	£63	£63
£12,200	Total CASH DUE IN	£508	£508	£508	£1,188	£1,188	£1,188
CASH DUE OUT							
£1,500	Mortgage	£125	£125	£125	£125	£125	£125
£900	Council tax	£75	£75	£75	£75	£75	£75
£1,250	Heat and light			£350			£300
£500	Telephone			£125			£125
£4,000	Food	£333	£333	£333	£333	£333	£333
£500	Clothes and cleaning	£40	£40	£45	£40	£40	£45
£300	House insurance	£25	£25	£25	£25	£25	£25
£150	Contents insurance	£13	£13	£13	£13	£13	£13
£1,200	Life assurance	£100	£100	£100	£100	£100	£100
£1,000	Motor/travel exps	£60	£60	£60	£60	£60	£270
£750	Entertainment	£60	£60	£65	£60	£60	£65
	Holidays						
£500	Sarah expenses	£40	£49	£45	£40	£40	£45
£100	Printing	£100					
£100	Stationery	£50		£10		£10	
£180	Postage	£15	£15	£15	£15	£15	£15
	Contingencies:						
£500	Repairs and renewals			£125			£125
£500	Sundries	£40	£40	£45	£40	£40	£45
£100	Office equipment	£100					
£14,030	Total CASH DUE OUT	£1,176	£926	£1,556	£926	£936	£1,706

(£1,830) (Excess of expenditure over income)

	Balance c/f	£332	(£86)	(£1,134)	(£872)	(£620)	(£1,138)

JOHN TAYLOR'S CASH FLOW FORECAST (months 7 to 12)

Budget		Month 7	Month 8	Month 9	Month 10	Month 11	Month 12
£1,000	Cash in hand	(£1,138)	(£886)	(£624)	(£892)	(£630)	(£383)
CASH DUE IN							
£1,600	Investment income	£133	£133	£133	£133	£133	£133
£2,300	Unemployment benefit	£192	£192	£192	£192	£192	£192
£350	Dependant allowance						
£7,200	Sheila (net)	£800	£800	£800	£800	£800	£800
£750	Richard	£63	£63	£63	£63	£63	£63
£12,200	Total CASH DUE IN	£1,188	£1,188	£1,188	£1,188	£1,188	£1,188
CASH DUE OUT							
£1,500	Mortgage	£125	£125	£125	£125	£125	£125
£900	Council tax	£75	£75	£75	£75	£75	£75
£1,250	Heat and light			£250			£350
£500	Telephone			£125			£125
£4,000	Food	£333	£333	£333	£333	£333	£333
£500	Clothes and cleaning	£40	£40	£45	£40	£40	£45
£300	House insurance	£25	£25	£25	£25	£25	£25
£150	Contents insurance	£13	£13	£13	£13	£13	£13
£1,200	Life assurance	£100	£100	£100	£100	£100	£100
£1,000	Motor/travel exps	£60	£60	£60	£60	£60	£130
£750	Entertainment	£60	£60	£65	£60	£60	£65
	Holidays						
£500	Sarah expenses	£40	£40	£45	£40	£40	£45
£100	Printing						
£100	Stationery	£10		£10		£15	
£180	Postage	£15	£15	£15	£15	£15	£15
	Contingencies:						
£500	Repairs and renewals			£125			£125
£500	Sundries	£40	£40	£45	£40	£40	£45
£100	Office equipment						
£14,030	Total CASH DUE OUT	£936	£926	£1,456	£926	£941	£1,616

(£1,830) (Excess of expenditure over income)

	Balance c/f	(£886)	(£624)	(£892)	(£630)	(£383)	(£811)

quarterly; car insurance and tax is usually paid six-monthly or annually. So after preparing the budget a cash flow forecast must be prepared.

John Taylor's cash flow forecast is on pages 36 and 37. It shows the opening cash in hand of £1,000 and the annual expenditure for each item divided into months, taking account of the variations in heating and lighting bills at different times of the year and the other bills which are paid for annually or six-monthly. The bottom line shows the forecast bank balance at the end of each month.

John will have to sell the family car by the second month because the forecast shows that, by then, his bank balance will be overdrawn by £86. And if he hasn't sold it by the end of the third month his overdraft will be £1,134.

The cash flow forecast needs to be updated every month, showing the actual income and expenditure for that month. It will immediately signal financial hiccups before they happen so that appropriate action can be taken to remove the worries of unexpected financial problems.

CHRIS WHITE'S BUDGET

As Chris's budget shows (see page 40), he is in real trouble, with an estimated excess of expenditure over income of £11,225, despite his plan to take a part-time job as soon as he can. Even if he puts the whole of his redundancy money towards the shortfall instead of investing half of it, he still cannot break even.

His first call must be to his local Job Centre, to discuss with them what help they can offer. It may be that they can assist with his rent and with the maintenance payments to his ex-wife. Almost certainly he will get a temporary reprieve from paying the council tax. The rules often change, so it is impossible to give specific advice—except that it should be asked for from the Benefit Agency at the earliest opportunity.

When Chris has the answers he will need to revise his budget accordingly. How dramatic these changes will be will depend on the help he can get with the maintenance payment, which is the major part of the shortfall.

The danger for Chris is that if, by planning ahead, his problems appear insoluble, he could panic, which would make it even more difficult for him to apply himself to finding the new permanent job he so badly needs. It is for this reason that the initial investment in a building society of part of his redundancy money is so important, because it provides a small income, it is not immediately available for 'panic spending', yet it provides him with a feeling of security knowing that it can be used for a real emergency, should one arise.

Once he has revised his budget he will need to prepare a cash flow forecast similar to John's and for the same reason. It will signal problems ahead and ensure that he keeps a check on impulse spending which is not allowed for in the budget and to which he may be prone.

SALLY FRASER'S BUDGET

Although Sally received only the statutory redundancy money to which she was entitled, her problems are not as serious as might be expected, even though her budget, set out on page 41, shows a shortfall of £570.

Her first call must also be to the Job Centre to sign on for unemployment benefit and to enquire whether she is entitled to income support and council tax relief. These benefits could well defray part of the shortfall.

Compared with Chris, a larger amount has been allowed in Sally's budget for clothes and cleaning, because it will cost her more than Chris to present a good appearance at interview, without which she will not find her new job. However, there is room in her budget for pruning here and there if she finds

BUDGET—CHRIS WHITE

Cash in bank	£0
Redundancy cheque	£10,000
Total capital	£10,000
Invested	£5,000
Cash reserve	£5,000

CASH DUE IN

Investment (say 8%)	£400(a)
Unemployment benefit	£580(c)
Part-time employment	£4,500(b)
Income support	(?)
Other benefits	(?)
Total cash due in	£5,480

CASH DUE OUT

Rent	£3,500(?)
Council tax	£300(?)
Heat and light	£500
Telephone	£400
Food	£1,000
Clothes and cleaning	£350
Contents insurance	£75
Life assurance	£0
Motor expenses/travel	£500
Entertainment	£350
Holidays	£0
Maintenance	£9,000(?)
Typewriter/files, etc.	£100
Printing	£100
Stationery	£100
Postage	£180
Contingencies:	
Repairs and renewals	£0
Sundries	£250
Total cash due out	£16,705

CASH DUE IN less CASH DUE OUT

Shortfall	(£11,225)

(a) 12 months   (b) 9 months   (c) 3 months
(?) Benefit?

BUDGET—SALLY FRASER

Cash in bank	£250
Redundancy cheque	£1,000
Total capital	**£1,250**
Invested	£1,000
Cash reserve	£250

CASH DUE IN (first year)

Investment (say 8%)	£80(a)
Unemployment benefit	£580(c)
Part-time employment	£3,500(b)
Income support	(?)
Total cash due in	**£4,160**

CASH DUE OUT

Rent	£750(d)
Council tax	£300(?)
Heat and light	£350(d)
Telephone	£200(d)
Food	£1,000
Clothes and cleaning	£500
Contents insurance	£50(d)
Life assurance	£0
Motor expenses/travel	£500
Entertainment	£350
Holidays	£0
Typewriter/files, etc.	£100
Printing	£100
Stationery	£100
Postage	£180
Contingencies:	
Repairs and renewals	£0
Sundries	£250
Total cash due out	**£4,730**

CASH DUE IN *less* CASH DUE OUT

Shortfall	(£570)

(a) 12 months   (b) 9 months   (c) 3 months   (d) Shared with flat-mate   (?) Benefit?

this necessary. Again, her cash flow forecast will give her fair warning of problems ahead.

*   *   *

Whether you are male or female, backed by a supportive family like John, on your own like Chris, single and sharing a flat in London like Sally, or your circumstances are different from any of these examples, the action you must take is the same.

First you must sign on for unemployment benefit and discover what additonal benefits, if any, you are entitled to; prepare a budget for the following twelve months; if there is a shortfall decide how it will be financed; finally, prepare a cash flow forecast to help you keep track of your financial plan and get fair warning if things start to go wrong.

If you are still in a job you will probably not have to budget so carefully to finance your job-hunting campaign, but even so you should work out your income and expenditure for the year and consider how your additional expenses will affect your cash flow. Like John, Chris and Sally, you will need to budget for a typewriter or word processor, stationery, postage and printing costs, and whether you can absorb these into your current outgoings will depend on your lifestyle and commitments. If you are at present saving nothing from your salary, you will need to see if you can cut down on any less essential items— for example, luxuries and entertainment. A cash flow forecast will help you to gauge when you are likely to be at risk of overspending—in fact it is a good idea to prepare one whether or not you are job-hunting.

On the next page there are some revision questions for you to answer. The alternative is to read through the chapter again to make sure you have remembered all the advice included in it.

Revision Questions, Chapter 2

1 If you are unemployed and do not intend going into business on your own, why do you need a business plan?

2 What is the most important part of your business plan?

3 Should you involve your family in your business plan?

4 What is the first step you must take as soon as you are
   unemployed?

5 If you receive a substantial redundancy payment, why
   can't it be used for expenses until you are employed again
   instead of going through the rigmarole of a business plan?

6 Suppose your total capital, including your redundancy
   money, is less than £1,000. Is there any point in investing
   it? Why not use it for your expenses until you are
   employed again?

7 There are two documents you must prepare for your business plan. What are they?

8 If the first of these documents shows that your estimated
   expenditure exceeds what you expect to receive, what are
   your options?

9 What is the reason for the second document?

10   How should you use the second document and what will
     it show you?

The model answers to these revision questions appear on page
185.

3 Working From Home

You can forget the word 'redundant' now, because you are working again: running your own business from home, which has one product to sell—YOU.

The past is now history and you are setting out on a campaign with the sole objective of finding the job you want. Not just any job. But the job you want. And this means a total commitment on your part and a determination to succeed. It demands positive thinking about your future.

Whether you are looking for a job by choice or because you have been forced into it is neither here nor there. All the same rules apply. The recommendations in this book are based primarily on the assumption that you are not working and that you can devote yourself full-time to your job-hunting campaign, but if you are currently employed you will need to make some changes to the time you allocate to it. The tasks you have to complete will be the same whether you are employed or not, and most of these will be undertaken at home.

WORKING FROM HOME

Working full-time from home needs a high degree of self-discipline—something which people who have never worked from home find very difficult to achieve at first. There are all kinds of distractions and endless opportunities to justify postponing or easing up on the more boring tasks.

So a rigid regime has to be established from the start.

You need to begin work at a set time each day, just as though you were going out to an office. The big advantage of working from home is that you don't have to join the commuter rush hour and wear yourself out before you get to your workplace—you just have to walk downstairs or into the next room. And therein lies a problem. It is so easy to stay in bed a little longer and then get up, put on a dressing-gown, make a cup of tea, and stroll into your 'office' and shuffle a few pages about. That works well for a few days, but it is no way to develop the self-discipline you will need when the going gets tough and you have to persist with your campaign even when you have had a longish period without success.

I have worked from home for more than twenty years and I soon realised the importance of a routine. It happens to suit me to start work early—at 7.30 a.m.—and to work through until lunch-time without a break. After lunch I like to take an hour or two off (especially in the summer) and then start again at 5 o'clock for a couple of hours or for however long I need. That routine certainly would not suit everyone, and it will be up to you to decide on your own work routine and stick to it.

Of course there must be flexibility in your routine because some days you will be going out to interviews, and on most days you will be spending time in your local library studying the papers for job vacancies. What matters is that you *start* each day at a set time. If you are going to work successfully from home you need all the help you can get, and a good start will carry you through the day.

You will need a base from which you can work. Ideally you

should have a separate room where you can shut the door and isolate yourself from the rest of the household—the spare bedroom is often the answer. But if you haven't got a spare bedroom or separate dining-room, establish your 'office' on a table perhaps in the corner of the sitting-room, or in the attic, or in your own bedroom.

If you are a family person, make it absolutely clear that you are to be left alone, undisturbed, during 'working hours', just as though you had left the house for the office. There is nothing more distracting than interruptions on domestic matters—and nothing more certain to provide an excuse to stop working, however self-disciplined you are.

As your campaign proceeds you will be gathering together all kinds of information. You will have copies of your CV; a ring-binder or two containing notes and copies of your applications for interviews and the outcome of the interviews you attend; as well as several files containing details and facts about the companies you contact. Keep this information together on your desk if you have one, or allocate a corner of a cupboard or a bookshelf where you can immediately put your hand on the information you want.

EQUIPPING YOUR OFFICE

During your campaign you will be writing several hundred letters of application, and as you will see when we study Chapter 12, I shall be recommending that your letters should be typed. Not only is a typed letter easier to read, but you will need to keep copies of the letters you send. It doesn't matter whether you are a typist or not. Most journalists are 'one-finger' typists and it is surprising how fast one-finger typing can be with a little practice. Even if you have never touched a typewriter or a computer keyboard before, now is the time for you to learn!

The ideal solution to your letter writing is a word processor

and printer, because you would be able to use it for your
letters; for compiling the information you will need for your
research; and for preparing your CV. If your budget will not
allow for expenditure on a word processor, then consider a
reconditioned portable electronic typewriter as an alternative.
A portable is particularly useful if you are short of desk space.

You will also need some stationery items.

I suggest you set up one or more loose-leaf files (A4 size)
in ring binders for the information and copies of letters you
will be accumulating. They need sturdy covers because they
will get a lot of handling. Loose-leaf binders are versatile and
enable you to index them and divide them into sections as you
add more information to them.

Apart from the binders, all you will need is a box of good
quality white paper (A4 size) on which to type your letters of
application, a box of 'flimsy' paper for your copies, some
carbon paper, and a box of white envelopes (DL size which
takes a piece of A4 paper folded into three). You will also need
some pads of ruled paper for your notes, and spare ribbons and
correction tapes for your typewriter.

With the development of computer technology and the ease
with which information can be passed down the telephone line,
more and more people, even with large companies, are working from home. Their computer terminal is connected to the
computer network in the office just as it would be if they were
working from their own room at the office.

The drawback for many people is that they feel isolated and
miss the company of their office colleagues. You have no
option and it is something you will have to get used to. However, once your campaign gets under way you will be spending
less and less time at home because you will be attending interviews; you will also be visiting the library to study the newspapers for job vacancies and to research the companies to
which you are applying. So any initial problems you experience
will not last very long.

So to summarise. Decide where you are going to set up your

home 'office'; establish your daily working routine; establish some 'house' rules while you are working; and buy the essential equipment and stationery items you need for your campaign. In the next chapter we shall study how the job market operates.

Some revision questions follow on the next page.

Revision Questions, Chapter 3

1 Is working from home as much of a problem as some people make it out to be? What are the real problems?

2 What is the first priority for working from home successfully?

3 On what other criteria does working from home depend?

4 What equipment and other items will you need?

5 What do you do if you can't type?

The model answers to these questions appear on page 187.

4 The Job Market

If you talk to ten different people on how to set about getting a job, you will get ten different answers. The principles will be the same but the methods will be different.

But that is exactly what you have got to do. You need to talk to as many people as possible who have experienced the same problems as you are experiencing now, and find out how they set about solving them, because you will soon realise that there are many different approaches to getting a job. It is not just a matter of writing hundreds of letters of application in reply to advertisements and depending on the law of averages. You have got to develop an approach which is right for you.

First, though, there are various aspects of the job market and job-hunting of which you must become aware. For example, did you know that some of the best jobs are never advertised? That advertisements do not always mean what they say? And that before starting to look for a job you have got to define your objectives precisely and decide on your own priorities—the relative importance to you of compatibility, salary and location?

What about the competition that you are up against? How serious is it?

Imagine a group of 100,000 people seeking a job, of whom

you are one. Each of these applicants is an individual with his or her own abilities and personality, and they are all out to sell themselves *against you*. That is a formidable challenge, but let's examine it in some detail and try to get it into perspective.

Of those 100,000 people, probably no more than ten per cent will be anywhere near the top of the list when it comes to getting an interview, let alone getting the job. And having got an interview, it has certainly never occurred to them that they have got to *learn* how to become an expert interviewee if they are to stand any chance of being offered the job.

Then you can break down that ten per cent still further into all kinds of skills, from administration to technical, from selling to buying, from accountancy to personnel, and so on. That has reduced the number of your competitors still further—you are no longer one in 100,000, you have already become a much bigger fish in a much smaller pond.

Many applicants are not seriously looking for a change of job. They may be applying for a number of reasons. They may want to check the market to see what other companies are offering for the job they do. They may be a plant for their company, indulging in a spot of industrial espionage to find out what the competition is doing. And some people even make a business of applying for jobs and living off the expenses they are paid for attending!

There are also those who do not really want to change jobs at all. They turn down offers for all kinds of reasons, such as the new job means moving to another part of the country and the domestic pressures against a move outweigh the benefits of making the change.

So, relatively few job applicants have learnt how to become skilled in job-hunting and many of them are not serious about changing their job anyway. All of which improves your prospects and helps to rationalise an apparently impossible task.

There are one or two other aspects of the job market and the way it works which you should be aware of before starting your own campaign.

It is estimated that less than 25 per cent of job vacancies are ever advertised!

What happens is this.

The personnel manager of a company is instructed to fill a particular vacancy. He draws up a job specification which describes the job in general terms—the person to whom the applicant will be responsible and a broad description of what the job involves. The job is advertised and will probably generate hundreds of replies. What happens to these replies and how they are processed will be described in Chapter 10.

Suppose three applicants, all equally qualified, are short-listed: there is only one job, so only one of them will be chosen and the personnel manager has the names of two first rate applicants still looking for a job. He will have friends who are personnel managers in other companies and he will ring round to one or two of them to ask whether they are looking for someone with the same qualifications. This could save them the cost of advertising their own vacancy and they may well be able to return the compliment at some later date.

The reason why many vacancies are filled without their being advertised at all is because people are 'passed on' from one personnel manager to another and personal contacts fill many job vacancies. It is called the 'network'. Anything up to 75 per cent of all vacancies are never advertised. The need to make personal contact is essential in any job-hunting campaign. Making contact, and techniques other than answering advertisements are discussed in Chapter 13.

Advertisements do not always mean what they say. You reply to an advertisement for which you are ideally suited. Your experience matches the job specification exactly. You get an interview yet you do not get the job. What happened?

Surprising though it may seem, the advertisement you replied to was for much more than the job described!

The company was looking for a person who not only meets the job specification now, but also has the capacity and ability to fill that job as it expands. They will also be looking for someone who can contribute to the profitability of the company and its future prosperity. All of those qualities may not apply to a person who can only meet the job specification as advertised.

Many advertisements for jobs appear to be so broadly based that almost anybody could do them. From the company's point of view that is not so absurd as it first appears.

Advertising is expensive, so if a company has got, say, three vacancies to fill, all with similar job specifications, the advertisement can be drafted much more loosely and it may be possible to fill all three vacancies with the one advertisement. This cuts the costs by two-thirds and makes a healthy contribution by the personnel manager to the company's profits.

How to analyse an advertisement and understand its true meaning, which is essential before replying to it, will be studied in detail in Chapter 11.

At the beginning of this chapter I mentioned that before starting to look for a new job you must be absolutely clear about your precise objectives and decide on the relative importance to you of compatibility, salary and location.

Is job satisfaction in a friendly atmosphere more important to you than salary? Are you hungry only for a high salary? Is location of prime importance? These are decisions you must take after discussing them with your family. There is no point in your saying yes to an ace job in the Outer Hebrides if your wife says she won't move because of the children's education or because she wants to be near her ailing father. If salary is a high priority, you may have to forgo compatibility or you may have to move.

It is most unlikely that all of these factors will come up in your favour at the same time, and it is much better to have a clear idea of the kind of job in which you will be happy and therefore more likely to be successful. Taking a new job is a big step, especially when it involves a move which will directly affect the whole family. So make sure you know what you are looking for and where your priorities lie, and then go for it.

There are some revision questions for you to answer on the next page.

Revision Questions, Chapter 4

1 'If you talk to ten different people on how to set about getting a job, you will get ten different answers.' That's a very good thing. Why?

2 On average, what percentage of job vacancies are advertised?

3 Why do companies sometimes turn down an applicant for a job, even though he or she exactly fits the job specification?

4 Why does a company sometimes advertise a vacancy with a job specification so wide that almost anyone could satisfy it?

5 Why do some people apply for a vacancy although they are not really interested in changing their job? Give as many reasons as you can think of.

6 If only a proportion of the job vacancies is advertised, how are the other vacancies filled?

7 What are the most important factors you must consider when changing your job? List these factors in their order of importance to you.

8 Amplify your reasons for the order of importance you

have given to the factors you have listed in the previous question.

9   Sum up the most important points made in this chapter to help you understand how the job market works.

The model answers to these questions appear on page 189.

5 Getting Into Training

Anyone who has studied this book and acted on the recommendations it contains can expect to take from three to nine months to find the job he or she wants and in that time will have written between 150 and 250 letters of application.

If that sounds a long time, how long will it take someone who has not appreciated that there is a great deal to learn about getting a job? Perhaps 18 months, two years, who knows? So what does getting a new job depend on and how does studying this book help?

Your first step, before you have any hope of getting near the top of a short-list for the job you want, is to become a *professional* interviewee. For every job you apply for you will be up against hundreds of competitors, but you can rest assured that no more than a handful of them will have done any training at all to improve their job-getting technique. So that will immediately give you a head start and reduce the competition substantially.

As I stressed at the beginning of this book, to become a professional interviewee you have got to get into training, just as you would if you were a runner entering a marathon.

The training is long and hard and is full of ups and downs. There will be days when you will be low, really low. There will be disappointments, days when your self-confidence will be at its lowest ebb. And then something good will happen—a phone call from an old friend you had forgotten about, who gives you a contact, someone to call. Or perhaps an interview goes especially well for you. At once your self-confidence is restored and the adrenalin starts flowing again. It is when you are low that the need for the self-discipline I referred to in Chapter 3 becomes all-important.

And now this may surprise you. Your objective is to get not one job opportunity on your desk but several. Ridiculous as that sounds when we all know how difficult it is to get one offer of a job, there is a good reason for it.

After a period of unemployment the temptation to take the first job which is offered is almost irresistible, even when you know the job is not right for you and at a salary below your salary bracket.

The reason why you take the job you don't really want is called panic.

A job taken under these circumstances will not last very long; within a few months you will be starting all over again, and everyone who has been out of a job more than once will know that the second time round is even tougher than the first.

On the other hand, if the job is very nearly right for you, and provided the salary is within your salary bracket, then take it. At the same time keep on looking for an alternative. If you are already in a job and looking for another one, you are starting from strength and not from the emotional strain of being unemployed. You will have more self-confidence and you will give a much better performance when it comes to interview.

But make sure that the salary *is* right.

If you take the first job offered to you at a salary of £3,000 per year less than you are worth, it will take you five years or more to get back to your starting salary, because no one will believe you are worth what you are asking.

So that is why you need to resist the temptation of taking

the first job offered and should aim to get more than one job
offer so that you can decide which one meets your priorities.
Perhaps one offers a better salary, but you will have to move;
another offers the challenge you are looking for, but the working conditions are unacceptable. And so on.

You may have to delay making a decision on one job if
another offer is on the way; I shall tell you how to deal with
this dilemma in Chapter 18.

The most obvious approach to getting interviews is by
answering advertisements (there are various other methods
which I shall deal with in Chapter 13), but perhaps the most
important route of all is one which many people who are
out of a job are reluctant to take. That route is to use your
friends and anybody you have ever known who will remember
you.

It is remarkable how people who are unemployed become
ashamed of it; they don't want anybody to know—some of
them still catch the same commuter train every day so that the
neighbours won't know they are unemployed.

When you are unemployed, all your prejudices must go—
to make way for a totally ruthless, self-centred and selfish campaign to get employed again. It's the one time when you must
use every means at your disposal, and that includes your
friends. You will be able to return the compliment when they
are in the same boat which, statistically, some of them surely
will be.

So, a CV—about which more in Chapter 7—must be on its
way to every one of your friends and contacts to make sure
they know that you are available. Maybe they won't be able
to help directly, but they all have contacts. If nothing else, this
will highlight who *your* friends really are!

And don't stop at using your friends.

You must talk to as many people as you can, whenever you
can. Don't be shy about striking up conversations—on train
journeys, for example, or on holiday. Conversations with
people you have not met before almost inevitably lead to 'what

do you do?', which is your opportunity for a spot of instant self-marketing.

The first step to being offered a job is an interview, and a vital ingredient in becoming a professional interviewee is practical training. You need interview experience. Most people who are out of a job, and many of those wishing to change jobs, will probably not have been interviewed for some years— some people like John Taylor, who have only worked for one employer, have no experience at all. Most unemployed people have very little experience of responding to an interviewer.

What is often not appreciated is that a good interviewer will have made up his or her mind about the suitability of an applicant in the first 90 seconds of the interview—the first 90 seconds of a 40-minute interview. So when you go to an interview you have got to assess your interviewer instantly and respond accordingly—and that needs practice.

When you are studying the newspaper advertisements you are no longer looking only for a job, you are looking for interviews, regardless of salary, location or type of job; you are looking for advertisements asking for people with exactly your experience and qualifications, so that when they get your letter of application they will certainly give you an interview. Your objective is to use that interview to practise selling yourself.

But more than that, you can practise assessing your interviewer. Remember that as you are going to be judged in the first 90 seconds of the interview, you have got to make an instant assessment of the interviewer and decide in a few seconds how you are going to respond in order to sell yourself. How you make this assessment and respond to the questions will be discussed in Chapter 15.

Interview practice will also help you cope with the problem of nerves.

There is absolutely nothing wrong with having nerves. On the contrary, if you do not have nerves you indeed have something to worry about. The person who claims not to be affected by nerves is either kidding himself or is totally insensitive and will fail at interview. We have all heard the star actor or actress being asked on a chat show whether he or she still suffers from nerves after years of first nights and stage experience. The answer is almost always 'yes'.

Nerves tell us that the adrenalin is coursing round our body because something special and of particular importance to us is about to happen. But to ensure that we give a good 'performance' we need to control them.

The first step is to be aware of how nerves affect you. They usually affect that part of the body which is about to be put under stress. So an athlete may suffer a tensing of the muscles; a singer will get butterflies in the stomach; a conjuror's hands may start shaking; a speaker may become short of breath or his mouth will go dry. Just when you want to remember all the good things about your previous experience your mind will go inexplicably blank.

Having identified how nerves affect you, the next step is to decide how to deal with them.

You will see the athlete, for example, shaking his legs before a race to loosen up the muscles. A singer or a speaker who suffers from breathlessness will do some deep-breathing exercises before the performance. In your case nerves are most likely to show themselves by a dry mouth, a shaking hand, or a mind that goes blank when you most need it.

The dry mouth can be dealt with by a glass of water, so if you are offered a cup of coffee or tea, opt for a glass of water instead, which is much more effective than coffee. If you know that your hands shake, rest them on the arms of your chair if it has arms. If not, rest them on the table or in your lap. Avoid gripping the arms of the chair as though you are at the dentist, because white knuckles will emphasise your nervousness rather than alleviate it.

If, as is most likely, your nerves result in your mind going blank, this will best be overcome by proper preparation for your interview (about which I shall have a lot more to say in Chapter 14) and by developing your self-confidence through interview practice. The more interviews you attend, the more your confidence will grow and the less you will be affected by nerves.

The message is to go out and get interviews. Get as much interview practice as you can, which will give you the confidence you need when you are being interviewed for the job you really want, and will greatly improve your chances of getting near the top of the short-list.

There are some revision questions on this chapter on the next page.

Revision Questions, Chapter 5

1 When you have implemented the recommendations in this book, you can reasonably consider yourself a trained job-hunter.
  a How long do you think it will take you (on average) to get the job you want?
  b How many letters of application will you have written?

2 What criteria must you consider to ensure that a job is right for you?

3 Why must you aim for more than one job offer before making a decision?

4 Is there any occasion when you should accept a job offer even when your criteria are not fully met? If so, when?

5 Forgetting averages (question 1), the length of time it will take you to get a job will depend on one factor. What is it? (You can answer this question in ten words.)

6 Should you ask your friends to help you find a job? If yes, how would you set about it?

7 As part of your strategy you must meet people who can help you find a job. Give examples of how you can do this.

8   To become a professional interviewee you need to get into training. How will you set about this training?

9   If you suffer from nerves at interview, should you be pleased or sorry? Why?

10   What is the first step you must take to cope with nerves? How will you cope with yours?

The model answers to these revision questions appear on page 191.

6   The Real You

In the next chapter you will be preparing your CV (your curriculum vitae), that vital document on which your success at getting interviews will undoubtedly depend. The CV will present your life history to date in a concise and easy-to-read form, giving only those facts which are relevant and in which the interviewer is likely to be interested.

It is easy to control what goes into your CV because you will be writing it. But when you get to interview, the interviewer can ask you any questions he or she wishes and may well decide to delve into your past history. Unless you are well prepared it is very easy to fumble when you are asked simple facts about your past which you have totally forgotten and may find it difficult to recall under the stress of the interview. To be asked details about your education, for example, and to be unable to answer them accurately, will not be in your favour.

Those of you who have had a medical examination for an insurance policy will remember the doctor asking for details of your parents' medical history and, if they are no longer alive, what age they were when they died, and what exactly they died of. Most of us find it difficult to recall facts like that, off the cuff. Nowadays insurance companies usually provide a check-list in advance of the medical, so that the applicant can attend the examination fully prepared with the answers.

The same preparation is needed for the interview—only more so because, in this case, prospective employers are unlikely to supply a check-list in advance. Even if they did there would be nothing to stop them asking questions which were not included on the list.

So very detailed preparation is essential, both for the writing of the CV and for the interviews which will follow.

On pages 69, 70 and 73 are three forms: the first is headed 'Your Education'; the second 'Your Career Details'; and the third 'Personal Evaluation'.

There will not be room for you to write down the information on the forms in the book, so draw them up on A4 size paper, using a separate sheet for each subheading. In Chapter 3, under 'Equipping your Office', I suggested that you set up ring-binder files for your notes. These pages will form the first section— an important section to which you will often refer.

YOUR EDUCATION

The information on these forms is for your own personal use— they won't be seen by anyone else—so make your notes as detailed as possible and, above all, be honest with yourself (this particularly applies to the Personal Evaluation form).

Although most employers will not be interested in your edu- cation before the age of nine or ten, for the purpose of your notes list all the schools you attended, with the dates you started and finished at each of them, starting with nursery school.

Note down your progress at each school, including your favourite subjects and those which you found difficult or uninteresting. (If you have kept your old school reports these will provide excellent memory joggers for both dates and per- formance.)

EDUCATION

What qualifications did you gain? Was there anything special about your school?
What were your best subjects?

FURTHER/HIGHER EDUCATION (Where appropriate)

Do you have all your certificates to check dates and grades obtained?
Were the courses you attended day or block release? Were they supported by your employer?

TRADE OR PROFESSIONAL QUALIFICATIONS (Where appropriate)

Were the qualifications gained by examination, age, experience, other qualifications, or a mixture of any of
these? Are you currently studying for anything else?

ADDITIONAL INFORMATION

What other activities were you involved in during your education - for example sports, membership of
school societies etc?

YOUR CAREER DETAILS

Most application forms will ask you to list your career in reverse order, showing your most recent employment first. Your job history (CV) should read the same way. Refer to any old correspondence you may have to check dates and use this page to list the jobs you've held. Alongside each job, list two major achievements and your reasons for leaving.

DATES	EMPLOYER	MAJOR ACHIEVEMENTS	REASONS FOR LEAVING

In particular, note down the examinations you took and the qualifications you gained.

You will need to record details of further education, if any, and find any further education certificates you have received which will enable you to check dates and the grades you obtained. The same applies to any trade or professional qualifications you hold, and you should note down whether these were obtained by examination or because of age and experience in your job.

Finally under the Education heading is a space for additional information. List any non-academic activities you were involved in at school such as sport, music, drama and membership of other special interest school societies.

YOUR CAREER DETAILS

The next form is for details of your career after leaving school and up to the present time. As with Education, this form needs to be completed accurately and in as much detail as possible. This may need some research because it is not always easy to remember the precise date on which you left one job and started another.

If you have worked for only one employer you probably held a number of posts as you progressed in the company. Treat each of them separately and record the same detail as though you had changed jobs.

Refer to old correspondence or pay-slips, bank statements or copies of tax returns. All of these will give you clues about dates, salaries and achievements.

The column headed Major Achievements is an important one. During your career there will have been many occasions when you had achievements which, at the time, you probably took for granted. In retrospect they may sometimes assume more importance and they may well provide useful ammunition at interview. Don't be put off by the word 'major'—any achievement which springs to mind is worth recording for future reference.

Be frank about your reasons for leaving a job. If you were dismissed say so and give the reason; remember these forms are for your own personal use, and how you use the information and present it will be up to you.

YOUR PERSONAL EVALUATION

Personal Evaluation involves you in some serious self-analysis.

The first section is called The Real You. What kind of person are you? Are you an introvert or an extrovert? Are you a charismatic person who gets everyone's attention as soon as you walk into a room? Or have you a more phlegmatic personality, preferring to remain, if not in the background, at least on the sidelines? What kind of temperament have you? Do you or don't you suffer fools gladly? Have you a sense of humour?

These and many other questions about you need answering. And probably the person least capable of answering them is you. We all have our role models and we know how we would *like* other people to see us, but to give an honest and objective self-description is sometimes difficult.

Test it out for yourself. Draw up a list of questions and ask someone you know reasonably well (but not too well) to answer the questions about *himself* and compare his answers with how you would describe him.

You can then use the same list of questions and listen to how he sees you. His answers can form the basis of your notes describing the Real You. But don't rely on the description of you by only one person. Ask several. Some answers will be common to all of them. Others will vary because people tend to tell you what they think you want to hear rather than give their honest opinion.

By studying the answers a true picture of the Real You

THE REAL YOU

Are you an introvert or an extrovert? Are you a good mixer? How would you describe your temperament? Are you superstitious? What sense of humour do you have?

HEALTH

What is your present state of health? Do you have any physical disabilities or limitations? Have you had any serious illness in the last five years? What is your height and weight?

HOBBIES AND INTERESTS

How do you spend your leisure time? What sports do you play? What clubs, societies or social groups do you belong to? Have you ever held office in any of them?

ADDITIONAL INFORMATION

What special skills do you have outside your normal job - for example do you have computer experience and if so, which system/software? What driving licences do you hold and are they "clean"? Do you speak or write any foreign languages? Have you travelled to any unusual places? Do you do any community work?

will emerge. Remember that the purpose of this exercise is to determine what the initial reaction of an interviewer is likely to be when you first meet, so you will need to know how to deal with your weaknesses and how to exploit your strengths.

You can learn quite a lot about yourself by analysing the reasons for your success or otherwise in the jobs you have held. You can often learn more from the jobs in which you were less successful than from those that went well. Was a lack of success due to your not having enough information to enable you to do the job properly—or was it because there was a personality clash between you and the boss? If there was an information gap, is that something which you can avoid in the future? If there was a lack of chemistry between you and your colleagues, whose fault was it, yours or theirs?

The more research of this kind you can do, the more accurate will be your final analysis of the Real You, and your strengths and weaknesses will become obvious.

The next heading on the Personal Evaluation form is Health. On occasions you will be asked to undergo a medical examination before you are employed and it saves time to have the answers to the questions which you will be asked readily to hand. Remember to include any information about the health of your family, and if your parents are no longer alive, note how old they were when they died and from what cause. The past history of your family's health provides the doctor with many clues about your own health now and its probable pattern in the future.

Next come Hobbies and Interests.

You will read in Chapter 7 how an interviewer will sometimes turn the conversation to your hobbies. This is not because he is particularly interested in hearing about your prowess as marbles champion of your prep school, but he will be looking for a common interest to help you relax. You will also need this information for your CV, so note the hobbies and sports in which you have been involved and how you spend your leisure time now. If you are a member of any clubs, societies or social groups, or have been a member in the past, note these down too.

Finally, there is a heading for Additional Information. This will list any information not included under the other three headings—foreign countries you have visited, for instance, any foreign languages you speak and whether fluently or just enough to order a meal—anything at all which will build up a complete history of your abilities, experience and interests. In short, a total picture of the Real You.

Get working on assembling the facts about yourself now. Many of them will be easy to remember, but you may have to do some research to fill in the gaps. You can't begin to prepare your CV, which is the subject of the next chapter, until you have completed the forms in detail, so don't be tempted to move on to the next chapter until you have done so.

7 Preparing Your CV

The dictionary definition of the curriculum vitae is 'an outline of a person's educational and professional history, usually prepared for job applications'. It is sometimes called a job history or a career record, but I shall be referring to it by the more generally used and understood term—the CV.

That it is the 'most important document you will ever write in your life' is without question, because it is an interview-getting document which has got to sell you on paper. You have written for an interview which is the first step in applying for a job and it is your letter of application and CV which will get that interview for you. So it is essential you get it right.

Everyone is an 'expert' when it comes to writing a CV. Indeed, there are people who advertise their services and undertake to write the 'perfect CV for you'. The fact is that there is no such thing as a perfect CV and there is only one person who can 'write a CV for you'—and that's you.

What I have done is to study many CVs and have talked to personnel managers about them. I have then extracted what I believe to be the best features from each of them in terms of content and presentation and combined them into one master CV which I am going to talk about now.

Before you go any further with this chapter, make sure you

have completed the forms described in the last chapter listing every detail of your life history and experience. You will be referring to them constantly.

YOUR SALES LITERATURE

If you were a salesman (which you are), you would either mail your customers or call on them with a sample of your product and printed literature describing it in detail. Think of your CV as your sales literature, which is selling your product—you. To pursue this analogy, think of the company buyer who receives your sales literature amongst hundreds of others from suppliers in his post every day. Most of it goes straight into the wastepaper basket. But some of it which looks easy to read may well survive.

Let's consider an 'easy read'.

What do you do when you get a form to complete? If it is well laid out and looks 'friendly', you will deal with it straight away. But if it looks complicated and forbidding you will probably put it to one side to deal with 'when you have time'.

A reader faced with hundreds of CVs will warm to the ones which look 'easy to read'; the others will be put to one side. Those that clearly need hard concentration or are hand-written and difficult to decipher will be dealt with much later— perhaps.

Whether or not a CV is an 'easy read' will depend on the content and how the content is laid out on the page. These go together so I shall deal with both of them in this chapter. But, first of all, here are some general rules about the content, regardless of layout.

SOME GENERAL RULES

In Chapter 10 we shall be discussing how the job selection process works and how a job vacancy is filled. We shall see that in most cases your CV and letter of application will be read first by an *eliminator* whose job is to find a good reason why you should *not* be called for interview and to reject your application. There must be nothing in your CV which will eliminate you.

Be positive. Avoid phrases such as 'I regret that I am not a qualified accountant, but I do have a very good knowledge of accountancy'. Negatives don't communicate—leave them out. Instead you will state positively what 'your very good knowledge of accountancy' amounts to.

When you are called for interview, the interviewer will have gone through your CV with a fine tooth comb and will have drawn up a list of questions. So whatever you include must not raise doubts or attract questions which you would prefer not to answer.

What is more, it must be factual, because if you are quizzed, in depth, on any part of it which does not stand up, or shows that you have bent the truth, it will throw the whole document and anything else you say into doubt.

An example of 'bending the truth' was a young man who came to see me recently and claimed to be a financial consultant; this surprised me because he was only 24 years old, which seemed young for a consultant. It turned out that he had worked as an insurance salesman for a few months and had been asked about the various insurance policies he was selling. It was true that he had been consulted about the financial benefits of the different policies, but it was pushing it a bit to describe himself as a financial consultant. That's what I mean by 'bending the truth'. Don't do it. If you have been an insurance salesman, say so—there's nothing to be ashamed of in that.

Don't mention pay in your CV or, as we shall see later, in your letter of application—neither what you have earned in the past nor what you want to earn in the future. After you have had some interview experience you may well change your mind about your pay bracket. You may want to lower your target, or you may want to raise it. Either way, if you have included pay in your CV, there will be a lot of them in circulation quoting the wrong figure.

Turn to page 82 where you will find the CV prepared by John Taylor based on the advice given in this chapter.

The aim is to contain the CV in not more than two typewritten pages. It can be presented in one page, the pros and cons of which I shall refer to in the next chapter. If it is more than two pages it will not constitute an 'easy read' and will be put to one side by most eliminators.

You must use A4 paper—that is the standard size of paper which 99.9 per cent of companies use. Foolscap paper is seldom used nowadays and is an irritation when it comes to filing because most filing systems are designed for the A4 size.

The CV which I am recommending is divided into six sections: Personal Details; Education and Qualifications; Career; Experience; General; and Aim.

Each of these sections (except the first one) is clearly identified by a side heading. Side headings are important because they immediately draw the attention of the reader to the section they are most interested in. Some readers, for example, may be more interested in Career and Experience than in Education. They can save time by going straight to those sections. The Personal Details do not need a side heading because these would normally head up the document.

JOHN TAYLOR'S CV

Let's analyse John Taylor's CV, line by line. Your CV can follow the same pattern because your objectives are the same although, of course, the details will be different depending on your experience.

Personal Details

The document is headed with the name you are usually known by and the title, which is Curriculum Vitae.

The details—name, address, telephone number, date of birth and so on—are typed centrally because this separates the left-hand column from the right-hand column and makes the information easier to read. Fast readers are used to grabbing information from a page by moving their eyes down the middle of it. Centralising the information makes it easier to do that.

In this section your name should be in full, even though you may seldom use your second or third forenames. Whenever possible restrict your address to only one line (you don't always need a house name *and* a street number, for instance). Give your home telephone number and, if you are still working and it is practicable, include a telephone number where you can be contacted during the day.

It is better to type your date of birth in full—in John Taylor's case, 10th August, 1954, instead of 10/8/54—it's that much easier to read in the longer form; then add your age in brackets, which saves the reader working it out and probably getting it wrong. Add your place of birth.

Marital status used to be no problem! You were either single, married or formerly married. But now that more and more people 'live with their partners', what should they say in their CV? My view, as always, is to be open and honest. If you say you are married but it transpires during the interview that you are not, the interviewer will wonder how much of the rest of your CV can be believed.

So, if you are single (regardless of whether you are living with a partner or not) say, Single. In this case your private domestic living arrangements are really no concern of the interviewer.

However, if you are single but living with a partner and have children, it is a little more difficult to describe your 'marital status'. Following the general advice of being truthful, I would

Name:	John Francis Tylor MIMI
Address:	4 Maple Street, Oxbridge. OB4 5BW
Telephone:	Home: 0865 723910
	Daytime: 0865 240399 ext.254
Date and Place of Birth:	10th August 1954 (40) Northampton
Marital Status:	Married – 2 children:
	Richard (18), Sarah (16)
Health:	Good – no disabilities

EDUCATION & QUALIFICATIONS

1965 – 1971	Westleigh Upper School, Northampton. 7 GCE 'O' Levels: Mathematics, Pure Physics, English Language, French, Geography, History, Commerce
1971 – 1974	Day release at Derwent College, Northampton. City & Guilds Certificates: Motor Vehicle Technicians – Parts I, II, and III Parts Administration – Credit Commercial Practice – Credit Motor Vehicle Electricians – Credit
1979	Elected Member of the Institute of the Motor Industry.
1994	I am currently studying for Membership of the Institute of Purchasing & Supply

CAREER

1971 – 1994	Oxford Motor Co. Ltd., Cowley, Oxon. (Manufacturers of saloon cars and light vans)
	Purchasing Manager (1987 – 94)

EXPERIENCE

Management

From 1977 to 1982 I was employed as a trainee manager gaining experience in various departments of the company.

In 1982 (age 28), I attended a 3-day parts purchasing course at Studley College and was appointed Assistant Purchasing Manager of electrical components with control of a stock of £450,000.

In 1987 (age 33), I was appointed Purchasing Manager responsible for the buying of all the Company's original electrical equipment, including batteries and accessories, with a budget of more than £1 million and a staff of 6.

Between 1987 and 1993 my stock levels increased to £2.75 million and my staff had increased to 10, consisting of 2 Assistant Buyers and 8 Clerical Assistants.

In 1994, my department was amalgamated with Engineering and Production and I was made redundant.

Engineering

My apprenticeship included experience in all departments of the Oxford Motor Company.

From 1974 to 1977, I was a Section Leader in the electrical workshop with particular responsibility for the making up of wiring harnesses.

Heavy Goods Vehicle Driving

I have experience of Heavy Goods Vehicles and in addition to my car licence I have an HGV Class I driving licence (both clean).

GENERAL

I am particularly keen on travel. As a student I hitch-hiked round the world and since then have travelled extensively in Europe. I am a keen golfer (handicap of 7) and photographer. My wife and I play squash regularly and I am secretary and treasurer of the Oxbridge Squash Club. We take an active interest in our local community activities.

AIM

I am seeking a job where I can use my management experience to contribute to my employer's prosperity and expecially to develop my experience of instilling loyalty and enthusiasm in the people for whom I am responsible. My wife and I own our house in Oxford, but now that our children have completed their early schooling we are willing to go anywhere.

---

still suggest that you should not say 'married', but say 'living with partner'. The fact that you have a stable 'family' relationship is a point in your favour and whether or not you are actually married is immaterial. If the interviewer wants to know more about your domestic arrangements, the subject can be brought up at the interview.

As for your children, it is enough to give their first names and their ages as John Taylor has done.

A word about health follows. If it is good, this must be in your favour. If, on the other hand, you suffer from any disability you should say so because it is bound to be raised during interview. You can add that your disability does not affect your work, if that is so.

Education and Qualifications

It is enough to give brief details of your education from the age of about 12—selectors are not interested in schooling earlier than that; include details of examination results and of any further education, together with degrees or qualifications.

Take care about educational qualifications when it comes to languages. To claim 'speaks French' as a qualification would mean to me that you are fluent in French, so I would try to get a fluent French speaker to interview you: you will feel a bit stupid if the interviewer suddenly asks you a question in French and you can't reply. So under this heading make it clear whether you are fluent or just have a good working knowledge of the language.

Career and Experience

There is genuine controversy about how the information under these two headings should be presented. Ask two personnel managers and you will get two opposing views.

The alternatives are, 1) to combine the two headings under *Career/Experience* and list your jobs with your experience alongside each one of them; or 2) to list your jobs under the *Career* heading and then summarise your experience under the separate heading of *Experience*, as John has done.

The problem with the first alternative is that if you have worked for several employers, doing a similar job for each of them, there will be unnecessary repetition alongside each job heading. If, on the other hand, you have had several jobs, all of them quite different (as was Sally Fraser's experience—see below) it is perfectly acceptable to list your experience alongside each of them, but this can give a disjointed picture to the reader of your true experience and abilities.

The second alternative has the advantage that you can highlight (by subheadings) your strengths and develop them as you wish. And if you have held a job which was a monumental failure you do not have to say so! Presenting your CV in this form does require a little more writing skill on your part, because it is much easier to describe each job you have held in three or four words than to summarise your work experience as a whole and present it in an easy-to-read style. But in my view it is well worth making the effort.

So to continue with our analysis of John Taylor's CV. He has had only one employer and he has cited his most recent appointment within the company which he will develop under the next heading.

Chris White (see page 14) who was also employed only by the Oxford Motor Company, would do the same except that he would add Training Manager and the dates.

Sally Fraser, on the other hand, had several jobs after leaving school and her entries under the *Career* heading would look like this:

1989–1994	Arkwright Advertising	Research Assistant
1988–1989	Lyncroft Advertising	Receptionist
1985–1988	Grants (Publishers)	Accounts Clerk
1983–1985	Arrow Bookshops	Junior Clerk
1982–1983	Moreton's Stores	Cashier

As you can see, Sally has listed her jobs in *reverse chrono-logical order*. This is because potential employers will want to know where she was *last* employed and, if that interests them, they will read on to what led up to it.

You must avoid gaps. They will stand out like a sore thumb to the reader, who will want to know what you were doing then (and where!). So if, for example, you took a year's sabbatical, say so.

And now comes *Experience*—this is the most important part of the document. John has decided that his strengths lie in Management and Engineering and so these become subhead-ings which, as part of the 'easy-read' rule, he underlines to draw the attention of the reader to them. Under these headings he summarises his experience, emphasising his strengths and, unless there is good reason to do otherwise, ignoring his weak-nesses.

He has added his Heavy Goods Vehicle driving experience not so much because he wants to become a long distance lorry driver but because a specialist qualification shows him to be versatile and it is something which other applicants might not offer. He could have placed it under a side heading of *Other Experience* if he had wanted to mention it but draw less atten-tion to it.

How you lay out this section will depend on your own experi-ence. Sally, for instance, would probably choose *Research* and *Administration* as two of her subheadings, emphasising her accounting experience under Administration.

In your summaries avoid any statement which you cannot substantiate. 'Experience of computer programming' sounds good, but unless you really have got that experience, don't claim it. As I have said before, always be truthful and factual.

Don't generalise. 'I was responsible for large stock-holdings in my last job' is nowhere near as impressive as saying, 'In my last job I was responsible for an inventory of 500 components.' 'I headed a department of 5 stock control clerks' is much more meaningful than 'I headed an important department'. You will be asked anyway, so quantify whenever you can in your CV. And use figures rather than spelling out the numbers in words—figures stand out from a document and look good.

General

The fact that John Taylor and his wife play squash regularly may seem a trifle irrelevant when it comes to a job application, but it is there with good reason.

When you go to an interview it is quite natural for you to be a bit anxious and tensed up. A good interviewer will not want to see you in a worried state—he will want to see you reasonably relaxed and giving your best performance. One of the ways by which he will try to achieve that is to pick out an item from that General heading, which has nothing to do with the job, and talk about it. In John Taylor's case the interviewer might ask him about that round-the-world hitch-hike he did in his teens, or about his golf handicap. He will find something in which there is a common interest which will help John to relax. The intention is not to put you off your guard so that you say something you don't want to say, but to see what sort of person you really are—the Real You, in fact. Travel is a particularly good subject to include if you can.

Aim

Keep this general so that it applies to any job you may be applying for; it rounds off the document and states quite simply what you are seeking. Apart from anything else it is a good exercise in that it will help you focus your attention on exactly what you *are* seeking. Make it clear that you will have the company's interest at heart as well as your own and that you will want to contribute to its prosperity, but make this sound sincere.

It is not a bad thing to say that you are willing to move, even if you are not. It shows flexibility, and after all, you may well have to move if you can't get a job without doing so. The word is 'willing', by the way, not 'prepared'. Prepared to move means you will only move if you are pushed into it and that will give a totally wrong impression.

A final point. Make sure your name appears on the second page of your CV, just in case the two pages get separated.

THE PROFESSIONALLY WRITTEN CV

What about having your CV professionally written for you? The newspapers are full of advertisements offering a CV service by 'experts'. By all means take advice on your CV, but let me say again—there is only one person who can write it and that is you.

A professionally written CV will stand out like a beacon to an experienced interviewer. The reason is obvious: the professionally written CV is usually 'word processed' from a databank of stock phrases selected to match your particular job experience and requirement. An interviewer quickly recognises the structure and content of the word processed CV. What he wants to see is what you genuinely believe about yourself and not the standard phrases which inevitably form the basis of the professionally written CV. He will also want to know whether you are capable of writing and presenting an easy-to-read document about yourself.

NOW WRITE YOUR OWN CV

Until now we have been analysing John Taylor's CV. Now you must write your own.

It will take you several days to get it right, and in between writing your drafts you can spend a bit of time revising some of the earlier chapters in this book. Try not to refer to the wording of John Taylor's CV when writing your own—yours must be an original document written in your own words. When you are satisfied with what you have written, go on to the next chapter in which I shall give you a check-list of what it should contain and then discuss how you should get it criticised and how it should be produced.

8   Producing Your CV

By now you should have what you consider to be the best CV you can produce—your own personal easy-to-read sales literature.

So let's run through it.

Starting with your *Personal Details*, you will have headed the page with your full name and then given: your address and telephone numbers (including where you can be contacted during the day if this is practicable); your date and place of birth (have you remembered to include your age in brackets after your date of birth?); your marital status, how many children you have and their ages; and your general state of health.

Under *Education and Qualifications* you will have given details of where you were educated from about the age of 12 and what qualifications you have. You will only have included qualifications which you can substantiate and this will particularly apply to foreign languages.

Under *Career* you will have listed your jobs in reverse date order, with the most recent one at the top of the list, and added the title of your last job in each employment. You will have made certain there are no missing years.

Then come details of your *Experience*. This will probably

have been the most difficult section to write. You will have decided which of your strengths you want to highlight and you will have used these as subheadings (for example, Management, Administration, Accountancy, Engineering, Personnel Management, or whatever) which you will have underlined to draw attention to them. If there are other attributes you want to mention without undue emphasis, you will have included them under a subheading of *Other Experience*.

You will have presented the facts about your experience in simple, easy-to-read statements. You can substantiate all the statements you have included in the summary of your experience. You will have avoided general phrases like 'I've had considerable experience in . . .' or 'I was responsible for a large budget in my last job'.

Instead you will have given facts supported by actual figures whenever you can: 'As office manager I and my staff of 6 were responsible for . . .' or 'I was one of a team of 5 in the Personnel Department and my particular responsibilities were . . .' or 'I was responsible for an annual budget of £250,000 in my last job . . .'

Under the *General* heading you will have included brief details of your hobbies or special interests which may have nothing to do with your job, but will provide the interviewer with a talking point to help you relax so that you give your best performance.

Finally, your *Aim* will have needed careful thought. What exactly are you looking for in your job? Certainly make it clear that you attach great importance to your contribution to the company's prosperity (but don't overdo it, make it sound sincere). Also make it clear that your own interests are important, too—otherwise you will not be believed! At the same time make sure that your aims are not so ambitious that they will eliminate you from any job for which you are applying because they sound unrealistic.

GET YOUR CV CRITICISED

When you have written your CV and believe that it properly reflects the Real You presented in an 'easy-to-read' form, the next step is to get it criticised by as many people as you can.

Your friends may remind you of something you did years ago which is well worth including but which you had forgotten about. Carefully analyse the comments you receive. You will not want to adopt them all. Indeed, some people will feel that a critical comment is expected of them even when they can find nothing to criticise, so some of the comments you receive may not be relevant. But it is well worth listening to as many comments as possible, even if only to ensure that you haven't left out something important or included something which may eliminate you.

PHOTOGRAPHS

Sometimes you are asked to send a photograph with your CV. It does not happen often, but if you are asked, make sure it is a *good* photograph. A professionally taken photograph will be worth every penny of its cost—passport photographs taken in a photo-booth simply will not do and may eliminate you before you ever get to the starting line.

The photograph need not be a head and shoulders passport type. One which shows you in a more relaxed setting—in the garden, for instance, or at your desk if you have one—will give a better impression of the Real You than a head and shoulders photograph. What is more, it will stand out from those of the other applicants, most of which are likely to be of the passport type.

MORE THAN ONE CV?

When you have a number of skills or your experience is broadly based and spans a wide range of subjects, there is a temptation to prepare more than one CV and use the one which is most appropriate for the job for which you are applying.

I wouldn't recommend it for the following reasons. If you have more than one CV there is always a risk that you will send the wrong one in answer to an advertisement. As we have already seen, some advertisements may cover more than one vacancy in a company, and if your CV is too specific you may eliminate yourself from an alternative opportunity. There is also the question of cost: the more CVs you have the greater will be the cost of producing them.

It really is much more practical to have one broadly based CV which is selling you and to use your letter of application, which we are coming to in Chapter 12, to expand and develop any aspect of your experience which is relevant to the job for which you are applying.

PRODUCING YOUR CV

It now remains to produce your CV.

If you have a word processor, a good quality printer, and you can type, you will have no difficulty in producing your CV using a layout similar to the one used by John Taylor (see page 82). Or you may have a friend who can do it for you. If not, go to a local typing agency and have it typed there, laid out according to your instructions.

If you find that what you have written will not fit comfortably on two typewritten sheets of A4 paper, go through it and edit it—editing will almost certainly improve your document anyway. It is important that your CV is contained in not more than two pages.

Then you will need 100 good quality copies. The agency

John Taylor - Curriculum Vitae

Personal Details

Name:	John Francis Taylor MIMI
Address:	4 Maple Street, Oxbridge. OB4 5BW
Telephone:	Home: 0865 723910
Daytime:	0865 240399 ext.254
Date and Place of Birth:	10th August 1954 (40) Northampton
Marital Status:	Married - 2 children: Richard (18), Sarah (16)
Health:	Good - no disabilities

Education & Qualifications

1965 - 1971	Westleigh Upper School, Northampton.
	7 GCE 'O' Levels: Mathematics, Pure Physics, English Language, French, Geography, History, Commerce
1971 - 1974	Day release at Derwent College, Northampton.
	City & Guilds Certificates: Motor Vehicle Technicians - Parts I, II, and III
	Parts Administration - Credit
	Commercial Practice - Credit
	Motor Vehicle Electricians - Credit
1979	Elected Member of the Institute of the Motor Industry.
1994	I am currently studying for Membership of the Institute of Purchasing & Supply.

Career

1971 - 1994 Oxford Motor Co. Ltd.
Cowley, Oxon.
(Manufacturers of saloon cars and light vans)

Purchasing Manager (1987 - 94)

Experience

Management

From 1977 to 1982 I was employed as a trainee manager gaining experience in various departments of the company.

In 1982 (age 28), I attended a 3-day parts purchasing course at Studley College and was appointed Assistant Purchasing Manager of electrical components with control of a stock of £450,000.

In 1987 (age 33), I was appointed Purchasing Manager responsible for the buying of all the Company's original electrical equipment, including batteries and accessories, with a budget of more than £1 million and a staff of 6.

Between 1987 and 1993 my stock levels increased to £2.75 million and my staff had increased to 10, consisting of 2 Assistant Buyers and 8 Clerical Assistants.

In 1994, my department was amalgamated with Engineering and Production and I was made redundant.

Engineering

My apprenticeship included experience in all departments of the Oxford Motor Company.

From 1974 to 1977, I was a Section Leader in the electrical workshop with particular responsibility for the making up of wiring harnesses.

Heavy Goods Vehicle Driving

I have experience of Heavy Goods Vehicles and in addition to my car licence I have an HGV Class I driving licence (both clean).

General

I am particularly keen on travel. As a student I hitch-hiked round the world and since then have travelled extensively in Europe. I am a keen golfer (handicap of 7) and photographer. My wife and I play squash regularly and I am secretary and treasurer of the Oxbridge Squash Club. We take an active interest in our local community activities.

Aim

I am seeking a job where I can use my management experience to contribute to my employer's prosperity and especially to develop my experience of instilling loyalty and enthusiasm in the people for whom I am responsible. My wife and I own our house in Oxford, but now that our children have completed their early schooling we are willing to go anywhere.

which types it may be able to produce these for you, or it may be more economical to go to an instant print shop which you will find in most high streets and which will produce the copies for you at a reasonable cost.

Make sure the copies are produced on a good quality paper. Flimsy paper easily gets torn or crumpled, so that by the time your CV reaches the 'boss', it will give a totally wrong impression of you.

Until now we have been considering a two-page typewritten CV. An alternative is to have the CV typeset and produced on one page. John Taylor's CV in this format is reproduced on page 95. The high street instant print shop could do this for you.

However, there is a difference of opinion as to whether the typeset format is an advantage. It may suggest that your CV has been professionally written. Although there is a positive advantage in having your CV on one page instead of two, I am inclined to the view that the two-page typewritten document is more personal and it will certainly cost you less to produce.

Once you are absolutely satisfied with your CV and have had it printed, you are ready to move on to PART TWO of this book and start your campaign in earnest.

Some revision questions follow on the next page.

Revision Questions, Chapter 8

1 When you have completed your CV, what step should you take before getting it printed?

2 What is the reason for taking this step?

3 What kind of photograph would you send if asked to do so?

4 Is there any advantage in having more than one CV? If not, why not?

5 What are the alternative methods of producing your CV?

6 What are the pros and cons of the alternative methods of production?

The model answers to these revision questions appear on page 193.

PART TWO
ACTION

9 Situations Vacant

Your preparation is complete with the production of your CV. You are now ready for action.

In this part of this book we shall be studying how to get interviews—that is your sole objective at this time. Then in PART THREE we shall study how to perform well at interview where your objective is to get to the top of the short-list and to be offered the job. If you have already started attending interviews you may want to go straight to PART THREE and read it now—then come back to this section.

The traditional way to obtain an interview is to answer an advertisement in the situations vacant columns of the press. There are other techniques which we shall be discussing in Chapter 13.

So where to begin?

Most of the leading national dailies run job supplements on a given day each week for a specific industry or profession such as Accountancy, Education, Media and so on.

You will be spending a lot of time in your public library from now on—not only in the immediate future when you are looking for advertisements to answer, but also later on when you are researching the companies you are applying to (more about that in Chapter 14).

You will need to go to the library every day. In the first week you must go through every newspaper every day and make a list of what supplements appear on what days and whether there is a general situations vacant column on the non-specialist days. Depending on the industry or profession in which you are interested or experienced, you will then know which papers you MUST see regularly. You may think some are worth buying each week, such as the *Daily Telegraph* (Thursdays) or the *Sunday Telegraph*. Others you can read on your daily visit to the library.

You must then add to your list the specialist journals and trade journals which cover your subjects. Again you will find many of them available in the reference section of the larger libraries. There is a complete list in a directory called BRAD (*British Rate and Data*). Some of these journals will be weekly, but most of them will be published monthly. Others are distributed on what is called a 'restricted circulation' basis and sent free to businesses in the industry they cover. They are not always readily available but it is worth phoning the publishers to see whether they will include you on their mailing list, or you may have friends in business who can get them for you. However you do it, you MUST see every newspaper and every journal which is relevant to your trade or profession.

If you are still in a full-time job, it will probably not be possible for you to visit the library every day unless there is a public library near your office where you can spend your lunch breaks. You may be able to visit your local library in the evenings, depending on what time you get home from work; otherwise you will have to go on Saturdays. During the week make a point of buying the newspapers on the days when they publish job vacancies that are appropriate for you. You will have to include this extra expense in your budget and cash flow (see Chapter 3).

Now that you know where to look, what are you going to look for?

You are looking for two kinds of vacancy. Obviously you

are looking for descriptions of jobs of the kind that you want. But you will remember that I said that, as part of your training to become a professional interviewee (Chapter 5), you need to get interview practice. So you are also looking for job vacancies where the specification matches your experience, even if the salary is lower than your target or the location is not where you want to live. At this stage practice is vital, even if the interviews do not lead to the job you want.

One drawback of doing your research in a public library is that when you come to write your letters of application you will need to analyse the advertisement in some detail (Chapter 11) and to do this you need it in front of you. Your options are to buy the paper which contains the advertisement or advertisements in which you are interested, or to make photocopies. Most of the larger libraries have photocopiers which you can use, but make sure the cost of photocopying several advertisements is not more than buying the papers in which they appear, which is much more satisfactory.

The daily search of newspapers and journals for advertisements can become a chore, especially when you can search for several days without any result at all, but it is absolutely vital that you maintain your search on a regular daily basis—even when it is raining and the public library is the last place you want to spend your time. If you miss a day you can be quite sure that it will be on that day that the advertisement you are really looking for will appear. Even if you see it a day or two later and make your application then, you are already trailing your competitors.

Now that you have your advertisements in front of you, you will need to analyse them carefully, not for what they say but for what they really mean. But before we look at how to go about this, it is important to have a clear idea of the procedure that companies follow when filling a vacancy.

10 How a Vacancy is Filled

Your route to the top of the short-list for the job you want is a long and sometimes tortuous one.

It usually starts with a letter of application, followed by a first interview and sometimes a second interview.

At each of these stages you will be up against intense competition and whether or not you succeed will depend on your giving your best possible performance. And that will depend to a great extent on confidence in your product—YOU—which will come from careful preparation for the interview and your interview experience. The more you know about how a company sets about filling a vacancy, the better equipped you will be to apply for it. So before we study the analysing of an advertisement and the writing of your letter of application, let's find out what happens when your letter of application drops through the letter-box of a typical medium-sized company. Even if their procedures vary in detail, the principles of advertising and interviewing are the same for all of them.

There are three ways in which a vacancy comes about—it can be because a *new* appointment has been created; or because two appointments have been *amalgamated*; or it can be an *existing* appointment made vacant by somebody who has left the company or been promoted. The procedure starts with a job specification.

If the vacancy is for a *new* appointment, the job specification will simply say 'responsible to . . . (whoever) . . . for . . . (whatever) . . .' There is no track record of the appointment so little else will appear in the job spec.

If, on the other hand it is for a replacement for an *existing* appointment, or where jobs have been *amalgamated*, there will usually be more detail about the responsibilities and what the jobs entail.

The job specification comes to the personnel manager. If more information about a new vacancy is needed, such as the proposed salary or more detail about the duties of the applicant, the personnel manager will consult the department head or the director who wants the vacancy filled.

The personnel manager will then write the personal specification. This has to take account of the guidelines laid down by the Equal Opportunities, Industrial Relations and Race Relations Acts. It will detail the experience and qualifications expected of the successful candidate; it may state an age bracket; and it will give the salary range, although sometimes, when it is a new appointment, the options may be kept open and it will say 'salary negotiable'.

Then the advertisement is written and placed in the newspapers or trade journals which the personnel manager thinks appropriate. If the company has an advertising department, it will be involved in the choice of journal and in the layout and preparation of the advertisement.

In due course the replies start coming in. There could be anything up to 300 or more replies to a single advertisement, and clearly the personnel manager could not read them all, especially if there are several vacancies being advertised at the same time. So members of the personnel department have been trained and given the responsibility of sorting them out. This has to be done as quickly and cost-effectively as possible.

These people will have drawn up a check-list by studying the job spec., the personal spec. and the advertisement—and, of course, they have a long experience of the company and a shrewd idea of the kind of person who will fit into each department.

They usually have three trays in front of them—one marked Rejects; another marked Possibles; and the third marked Probables.

They read the letters and mark each one out of ten: scores of seven or more go into the Probables tray, scores of less than seven and more than three go into the Possibles tray—all the rest go into the Rejects tray. These people are the first hurdle you have to overcome. But what you must realise is that they are not looking for someone to fill the vacancy. They are looking for applicants who couldn't possibly be suitable. They are the *eliminators*. They are reducing the number of applications to a manageable level.

Fortunately for them, there is always a large group of applicants for any job which automatically eliminates itself. Some personnel managers call it the 'lunatic fringe'. It includes people who apply for jobs which are clearly outside their salary range, and people who cannot be bothered, or perhaps have never learnt, how to write a letter of application. They write: 'I've read with interest your advertisement and I am confident that I can do the job to our mutual satisfaction—full stop—end'. Pre-empting the personnel manager's decision is not a good way to start . . . Or they say: 'I've read with interest, etc. . . . please see my CV attached . . .' On the face of it that makes sense; but if you think about it, why should the eliminator do your work for you and wade through the CV to see whether there is any good reason to put you into either the Possibles or the Probables trays? It is up to you to provide that information in as concise a form as possible in your letter of application (more about that in Chapter 12).

The letters in the Probables tray are handed to the personnel manager who will read them and decide whether or not to send an application form if that is what the company requires.

Otherwise they will be passed on to the head of the department whose vacancy it is.

Depending on the number of applications, the personnel manager may also read some or all of the Possibles to make sure the eliminators are doing their job properly—that they are not eliminating people who should be classified as Probables. Some of the Possibles may also be sent an application form.

In this way the 300 or more applications have been reduced to, say, 100 Probables and Possibles, of which some 50 or so will be sent an application form. Some companies send the Rejects and failed Possibles and Probables a standard letter of acknowledgement and 'regret the vacancy has been filled', but this is the exception rather than the rule. As you will discover, more often than not, you will get no reply unless you are sent an application form or invited to attend an interview.

Clearly, if you are applying to a small company without a personnel department, the procedure may be different, but the principle will be the same. For example, the managing director's secretary may well act as the eliminator before passing on the Probables. Whatever the internal system, it will not affect the way in which you write your letter of application.

So you see the importance of your letter of application and why it must not contain anything which may eliminate you. It is just as important as the CV except that, instead of being a standard document which you will be sending to everybody, it will be tailored to match what you have understood the company is looking for from their advertisement. Your letter must end up in the Probables tray.

There are some questions on the next page which you may care to answer to make sure you have a clear picture of how a company fills a vacancy. Alternatively, you may prefer to read the chapter through again before continuing.

Revision Questions, Chapter 10

1 In how many ways can a vacancy be created in a company? What are they?

2 There are two specifications for every job. What are they?

3 Who prepares the two specifications and what do they contain?

4 When the replies start coming in, who deals with them? What are they looking for?

5 What happens to the letters after they have been read?

6 Give examples of why some letters of application are rejected by the readers.

7 What's the 'lunatic fringe?'

8 What happens after the letters have been sorted?

9 Suppose the company doesn't have a personnel department, what happens then?

10 Under no circumstances must your letter of application contain anything which may '———— ————' What are the missing words?

The model answers appear on page 194.

11 Analysing an Advertisement

In Chapter 9 I said that advertisements for jobs do not always say what they mean; sometimes, too, they are not very well written and it is difficult to know exactly what they do mean.

You have probably already been studying job advertisements and applying for interviews and have been disappointed by the lack of response to your letters. Unfortunately, but perhaps understandably, companies do not always acknowledge the hundreds of letters of application they receive in response to an advertisement, especially those which end up in the Rejects tray.

In the last chapter we saw that your aim is to get your letter of application into the Probables tray. This will depend on the content and layout of the letter which we shall be studying in the next chapter. But the content must show that you have fully understood what the company is looking for and that you are the person who can meet their need. You must therefore read between the lines of an advertisement and try to determine exactly what they want. You won't always get it right, but when you do you will greatly increase your chance of getting into the Probables tray.

On page 112 is an advertisement for a company buyer which interests John Taylor because of his previous buying

Company Buyer

**Excellent
promotion
prospects**

Applications are invited for the post of Company Buyer for Eastling Enterprises, the Stationery Supplies Division of ABC Distribution plc., based in Herne Bay in Kent.

This is a rapidly expanding supplier of stationery products and has 250 employees. The appointment is for a Buyer with sound negotiating and purchasing experience.

The successful candidate will be responsible to the Chief Buyer for the purchasing of a new range of specialised stationery products and will have had at least five years buying experience with a major company, preferably in stationery although this is not essential.

The ability to work under pressure and be capable of taking decisions is essential.

☐ There are excellent promotion prospects within the Group.

☐ Age range is 25/40.

☐ Salary is negotiable.

A letter of application containing brief details of experience and qualifications should be addressed to:

The Group Personnel Director,
ABC Distribution plc.,
ABC House,
London, W1P 3VV

Eastling ENTERPRISES

The stationery business moving forward

experience. In this chapter we shall study how he should analyse this advertisement before replying to it. You can then apply the same principles to advertisements which interest you.

For the purpose of this exercise, assume that you are John Taylor with his experience—you may want to reread his CV in Chapter 7 to remind you of it.

What is the advertisement for? Yes, I know it says company buyer. But if you look at the specification carefully it becomes clear that what they are probably looking for is a purchasing director.

'The appointment is for a Buyer with sound negotiating and purchasing experience.'

'The ability to work under pressure and be capable of taking decisions is essential.'

These are clues to the fact that Eastling Enterprises, which is expanding—it says so—wants to bring in a buyer now at, say, £18,000, see how he gets on, and hope he will be capable of expanding with the company and take over purchasing responsibilities at £35,000 in five years' time.

The company is in stationery supplies. Do you want to work in stationery? A bit different from what you have been used to. Could you use your experience in buying electrical components to buy stationery? You probably could because there will be a large inventory of small items which is what you have been used to, so the stock control problems are likely to be similar. Before going to interview you will need to do some research into the suppliers of the stationery market, so that you can show your willingness to learn about the market and apply your previous experience of negotiating to it.

The company is called Eastling Enterprises which you have probably never heard of, but it is part of ABC Distribution plc—a quoted company. So you must check the share price in the *Financial Times* and find out all you can about the ABC Group—is it on the way up or on the way down? If it is on the way down you may find yourself unemployed again in a year's time. You will learn more about researching companies in Chapter 14 when you are preparing for your first interview.

It is based at Herne Bay in Kent. You live in Oxbridge. The personnel manager will undoubtedly say to you, 'I see you live in Oxbridge. We're based in Kent—what will you do about that?' You must have your answer ready. Will you move or stay locally during the week and travel home at weekends? You must have your answer ready because you are sure to be asked the question. A hesitant answer may eliminate you.

The company has some 250 employees. Now, that is interesting. The figure of 250 employees would appear to be high for a company supplying stationery items. One possible answer could be that they buy items in bulk, break them down and repack them in small quantities for supply to retail outlets or even direct to the public. A chat with a local retail or wholesale stationer may throw some light on the company and how it operates.

Next comes the job specification. 'The successful candidate will be responsible to the Chief Buyer for the purchasing of a new range of specialised stationery products . . .' It would be worth finding out what 'specialised' stationery products are. Again, call on your local stationers and ask them whether they buy from Eastling Enterprises and if so, what?

And now the personal specification: 'The successful candidate . . . will have had at least five years' buying experience with a major company, preferably in stationery although this is not essential.'

Experience in stationery is not essential—that suggests that they have been having trouble filling this job; initially they would not have said experience in stationery is not essential. You haven't had experience in stationery, but you can certainly show how the buying of a wide range of electrical components for the motor industry is similar. It involves the stock control of a wide range of small items and the need to avoid tying up large sums of money by making the range too wide. You will need the same negotiating skills. All you will have to learn is who the suppliers are and the price structure.

The candidate will be between 25/40 years of age. Now let's get this age bogey out of the way. You are just over 40. Other people reading this advertisement could be older, say 44 or 45, and they don't apply. That's ridiculous. Look at the age span of 25–40—that's 15 years and cannot be meaningful—another clue perhaps that they have been having trouble filling the vacancy. How did they arrive at it? Well, they want someone with five years' experience so the applicant can't be much younger than 25, and if they are looking for someone with some years to go and perhaps become purchasing director in five years' time, he shouldn't be more than about 40 now—but, of course, these age limits are flexible and they are not going to turn down an ace candidate just because he is 45.

'The ability to work under pressure and be capable of taking decisions is essential'. Doesn't that suggest to you that what they are looking for is someone who is more than just a buyer of a range of stationery products—someone who can expand with the business, contribute to its prosperity and take over the department in due course?

'Salary is negotiable'—another clue that they are having a problem with the vacancy. Analysing an advertisement in this way is going to help you, not only with your letter of application, but also at interview. It is very impressive at interview to show that you have thought about the job beyond the words of the advertisement. Even if some of the conclusions you have drawn are not totally correct it shows that you are a thinking person.

Now, find some advertisements which are appropriate to your experience and analyse them in the same way as we have analysed the advertisement in this chapter. Write down your analysis and note how your own experience relates to your analysis. Repeat the exercise with several advertisements. The more you analyse the more expert you will become in recognising what the advertiser is really looking for and the easier it will be for you to write your letter of application.

When you have done so, and before reading the next

chapter, write a letter of application in response to one of the advertisements you have analysed. In the next chapter we shall be studying the letter of application and you can compare the advice given with the letter you have written.

12 Your Letter of Application

On page 118 there is a final draft of John Taylor's letter of application in response to the advertisement which we analysed in the last chapter.

Many drafts preceded it and no doubt you made several attempts at the letter you have written in reply to your chosen advertisement before you were satisfied with it. Have it in front of you while you read this chapter.

Every letter of application you write will, of course, vary a little from the last one because you will be tailoring it according to your analysis of the advertisement to which you are responding. However, the structure of the letters will remain the same and will conform to some simple rules. At all times remember the purpose of the letter is to get an interview and that, in the first instance, it will be read by an eliminator who is looking for reasons why you should *not* be included. Your letter must end up in the Probables tray or, at the very least, in the Possibles tray. It will not get you the job—that will come only from the interview which should follow it.

Imagine the situation which was described in Chapter 10, 'How a Vacancy is Filled'. The eliminator has a pile of letters on the desk—some handwritten, some typewritten, some on large sheets of paper, some on small bits of 'domestic' size

4 Maple Street
Oxbridge OB4 5BW
Telephone: 0865 723910

Mrs Jayne Wilson
Group Personnel Director
ABC Distribution plc
ABC House
London
W1P 3VV

17 June 1994

Dear Mrs Wilson,

Company Buyer - Eastling Enterprises, Herne Bay - reference DT15

I wish to apply for the vacancy you are advertising in today's Daily Telegraph. The department I was managing for my previous company has been amalgamated with another and a senior colleague has been appointed manager of the combined departments, resulting in my being made redundant.

For the past 12 years I have been employed in the buying department of the Oxford Motor Company at Cowley. Seven years ago I was appointed manager of the department responsible for buying a range of some 3000 electrical components. My annual budget for last year was £2.75 million. I had a staff of 10 people and during this period gained a reputation for hard negotiating with our suppliers. I believe I could readily apply my experience to stationery buying.

A move to another part of the country would present no problems. I look forward to meeting you and having the opportunity of expanding on my experience.

Yours sincerely,

John Taylor

John Taylor

letter paper, some on a single sheet, some on two or more sheets. Some of them will be an immediate 'easy read', but a lot of them will need effort on the part of the reader. The eliminator will first sort the letters into two piles—one of single easy-to-read sheets; and the other, the 'difficult' ones which may be read later or be consigned unread to the Rejects tray.

So the first rule is that your letter must occupy no more than a single sheet of A4 paper.

And the second rule is that it must be typed. A typewritten letter is much easier to read than a handwritten one and the reader will be used to reading typescript. But even more important than that: you will need a copy of the letter, so that when you attend an interview some weeks later you will know what you said in your application, which the interviewer will have in front of him. Firmly attach the advertisement to your copy of the letter so that you can refer to that, too.

File the copies of your letters of application in your ring binder so that you can find them when you go for interview. Remember you are probably going to end up with a hundred or so letters, so you must have some system for finding them easily.

And now some simple rules for the layout of your letter.

If you haven't got printed letter-heads, start with your address and telephone number at the top of the page.

Next you must decide to whom you are writing. In the sample advertisement to which John Taylor is replying it says write to the Group Personnel Director at the London address. Find out that person's name by telephoning the company and asking— 'I want to write to the Group Personnel Director, will you tell me his or her name, please'; usually the telephone operator will tell you. Make sure you know how it is spelt—our name is our most precious possession and we like to have it spelt correctly.

Then type in the name, title, and address of the person to whom you are writing. Next comes the date, written in full as shown in the example.

You can now start the letter with Dear Mrs Wilson or Dear Mr Brown, as the case may be. It will be a point in your favour that you have taken the trouble to find out who the Group Personnel Director is. But if you are in any doubt about the name—or how it is spelt—then start the letter with Dear Sir or, if you know the person is female, Dear Madam.

Put a heading to your letter, such as 'Company Buyer—Eastling Enterprises, Herne Bay—reference DT15'. It could be that the company is advertising for staff at more than one location, so it is important that your letter gets to the person who is dealing with the vacancy in which you are interested.

The reference DT15 or whatever is included if you are asked to do so in the advertisement. (In fact no reference is asked for in the Eastling Enterprises advertisement.) A company will often advertise a vacancy in different papers. When your reply comes in, a copy will be taken and sent to the media department who will record what replies come from what paper. So next time they will know which paper gives the best results. Your telling them where you saw the advertisement helps them to improve their advertising response rate.

And now the all-important content. It must be concise and to the point. It will usually comprise three paragraphs, as in the example—let's go through them one by one.

Paragraph One
A few lines explaining why you are seeking a job. In the case of John Taylor he would say something on the lines of '. . . when my department was amalgamated with another, the senior manager took over and I was made redundant.' There is nothing to be ashamed of in being made redundant, especially when the reason can be explained.

If you are still employed but wanting a change, say so, with a brief comment giving the reason—you 'want a job with more responsibility' or you 'want to move to Kent (or whatever)'.

If, on the other hand, you were sacked for incompetence,

you will have to be careful and it may be better not to mention it in the letter, but prepare to deal with it at interview. You are certain to be asked.

Paragraph Two

This is the important paragraph. Here you must match your skills and experience as closely as possible to those asked for in the advertisement, referring to the notes you made when you analysed it. John Taylor has had 12 years' buying experience for a major motor manufacturer. He has been concerned with electrical components, which has given him experience of buying a wide range of products. He has been in a highly competitive industry, so his negotiating skills were of paramount importance in the contribution he made to his company's profits.

   You will have entered much of the information you will need for this paragraph on the forms you completed in Chapter 6 when you were recording facts about the Real You and your job successes.

   Of course you won't match all the criteria listed in the advertisement, but match as many as you can. The reader of the letter will think this man or woman is worth interviewing— and remember that is the purpose of the letter. So you will notice that everything in John Taylor's letter is positive. He doesn't say: 'I regret I have had no experience in the stationery industry, but . . .' That's a negative statement and negatives don't communicate. Of course it will come up at interview, but more about how to deal with that in Chapter 16. This letter of application must contain only positive reasons why the company should interview you. The words 'not' and 'don't' must never appear.

Paragraph Three

Your concluding paragraph. Say that you are willing to move if necessary (you may have no choice if you really want the job) and end up with something like 'I look forward to your reply' or 'I look forward to meeting you and expanding on what I can offer you', which rounds off the letter.

If you have started the letter with 'Dear Mr Brown', then end it 'Yours sincerely'. If you have started it 'Dear Sir', end it with 'Yours truly' which sounds less impersonal than 'Yours faithfully'.

Leave a space for your signature and type in your first name and surname. Don't use capital letters for your name which always look arrogant. Just normal upper and lower case, as printers would describe it. The reason for typing your name is simply that many of our signatures are illegible to anybody but us and you want to be sure the company knows your name.

By the way, do remember to sign the letter. Sometimes people forget and there is nothing more incomplete and certain to be rejected than an unsigned letter.

Then post it—some people forget that, too!

When the advertisement asks you to apply to so and so (the Group Personnel Director in the example we have been studying) enclose a copy of your CV with the letter. If the advertisement asks you to send or telephone for an application form, wait until you have received the form and enclose the CV with it.

I cannot overstress the need for you to remember that the *sole* purpose of this letter is to get you an interview. It is one of hundreds of letters received by the company and the more concise it is, and the easier it is to read, the greater will be the chance of it ending up in the Probables tray.

So how do you rate the letter you wrote before you read this chapter? It probably needs some work on it. It is a worthwhile exercise to write a number of practice letters in response to advertisements, even when you don't want the job, and to put them aside for twenty-four hours. Then read them, but this time put on the hat of an eliminator and read your letters objectively. It is much easier to criticise your own letters the following day than immediately after you have written them.

Some of your letters will fail, however good they are. You

won't win them all. But by following the advice in this chapter you will greatly increase your chances of getting a reply.

THE APPLICATION FORM

Having written your letter of application you will: 1) be invited to an interview; 2) be sent an application form; or 3) at worst, hear nothing.

There is little to say about application forms. There are well designed ones and badly designed ones. Either way they include questions which you must answer as accurately as possible. If it is practical to type your answers, do so, because it will be easier to read; with some forms it simply isn't possible, in which case write as clearly as you can.

You will need to keep a copy of the form including your answers so that you can refer to them before an interview. Get it copied by a photocopying service in your local high street or at the public library. File this copy with your letter of application and the original advertisement.

In the form you will be asked for details of your career to date and it will often say that if there is insufficient room, continue on a separate sheet of paper. That is your opportunity to say: 'I am attaching a CV which gives full details of my career and experience.'

References

If you are asked for names of referees you must, of course, give them.

The problem arises if you are still employed and do not wish to give your present employer's name. In this case you will have to explain why you are not giving his or her name and offer other references from people you have worked for in the past or who know you well.

Ask the persons concerned for their permission to give their names. You don't want them getting a request for a reference out of the blue and, if you know them well enough, it is as well to find out what they will say about you.

You should now be sending out letters of application regularly and some of these will result in your being asked to attend an interview. I shall deal with the first interview in detail in Chapter 16, but there are other methods of marketing yourself apart from answering advertisements, and these are the subject of the next chapter.

13   Other Self-Marketing Techniques

The usual way to get a job is to apply for an interview by replying to advertisements in the national and in the trade press. But there are other techniques which should be included in your job-getting campaign.

In Chapter 5 I recommended that you should use your friends and indeed anybody you have ever known who might have contacts who could help you. It is called the network and, as we saw in Chapter 4, about three quarters of job vacancies are filled by the network, or by being passed on from one personnel manager to another.

You must write to them all explaining what has happened to you and enclosing a few copies of your CV. They may not be able to help you themselves, but they have friends and contacts to whom they can give a copy of your CV. You may well end up being interviewed by a company that you have never heard of.

Some people feel embarrassed about using their friends in this way—they feel they are imposing on them—but when you are out of a job you cannot afford to feel embarrassed, and if they are real friends they will want to help. If they are not real friends, it doesn't matter if they do feel imposed upon. After all, as I said in Chapter 5, statistically some of your friends may well be out of a job themselves in the future and then you can help them. So exploit personal contacts to the full—that's how most job vacancies are filled.

Then there are what are called 'round-robins'.

These involve reading the business pages of the national press, the *Financial Times* and the trade press, and writing to companies you would like to work for and where you believe you have the skills or experience which would contribute to their business.

Write to the personnel director or managing director on the following lines: 'I see from a report in the *Financial Times* that you are planning an expansion. I would like to be part of that expansion because I have experience of (whatever) and believe I could contribute to your development.'

You will need to research the company—I shall be saying more about sources of company information in Chapter 14— to find out as much as you can about it so that you know what it does and where you could fit in.

Write to as many companies as you can on those lines. And if, indeed, the company is intending to take on more staff, your letter could save them money by relieving them of the need to advertise the vacancy.

Then, of course, you must register with the employment agencies. There are many of these: some are general agencies which cover all types of businesses and others are specialist agencies concentrating on a particular industry or profession. You will find the names of agencies in your locality listed in the *Yellow Pages* and in the job advertisement pages of your local paper. There are also various directories, which should be available in the library, such as the *Personnel Manager's Yearbook* which contains a list of agencies throughout the country.

Select those agencies which appear to cover the fields in which you are interested, and which are likely to have on their books clients who could use your skills and experience.

Write to them explaining that you are looking for a job and

enclose a copy of your CV. They will probably want to interview you. Once they have your details on their computer they can marry these up with requests from a client to find a suitable applicant for a vacancy.

If a vacancy arises they may then want to interview you again so that they can compile a short-list of probables for their client. In this event your first interview with the company may be the only one and you should ask how many interviews there will be so that you will know how to respond to it (more about responding to first and subsequent interviews in Chapters 16 and 17).

The agency should receive its fees from the employer, but do confirm beforehand that no charge will be made to you.

Finally, always have copies of your CV with you. You could be travelling on a train, for example, and it is not difficult to get into conversation. Inevitably the talk will turn to what you do, and that is your opportunity to say that you are just changing your job; even if the person you are talking to cannot help, he may know somebody who can—so give him a CV!

You must be ready to grab any opportunity to market yourself. Most of us are inhibited when it comes to selling ourselves into the job market and tend to underrate our abilities. There is no place for these inhibitions when it comes to job-hunting.

This ends this part of the book and there are some revision questions on this chapter on the next page.

By now you should be getting interviews—even if only practice ones. If you are going to get to the top of the short-list you have got to perform better than your competitors at these interviews. Think of them as sales presentations. There are two parts to any sales presentations. The first is demonstrating the product and the second is closing the sale. How to apply these same principles to yourself will be fully dealt with in PART THREE of this book.

Revision Questions, Chapter 13

1 What is the 'network' and how are you going to use it?

2 What are 'round-robins' and how will you use them?

3 How will you find out which employment agencies to contact?

4 What, in particular, do you need to know from an agency before you attend an interview with one of its clients?

5 What should you confirm with the agency before committing yourself to it?

6 Are there any other occasions when your CV can come in useful?

The model answers to these questions appear on page 196.

PART THREE
CULMINATION

14 Sources of Company Information

By now you have probably attended some interviews—the last stage in getting a new job. No doubt you have thought about how they went and wondered whether you could have 'performed' better. The third part of this book deals with every aspect of the interview, from confirming that you will attend until you are offered a contract to sign.

Before you attend any interview, however, you have some preparation to do. You must find out as much about the background of the company as you can. Not only will this give you confidence at the interview, but the interviewer will be most impressed by the fact that you have taken the trouble to research the company in advance. It will be very much in your favour. This chapter tells you how to set about it.

Company records are kept at Cardiff, but it is still possible to carry out a company search in centres in the main cities of the United Kingdom. It will be presented to you on a microfiche which can be viewed at the centre. However, a company search will not necessarily provide you with the information you need for the interview. In any event, you will have to be capable of interpreting company accounts and audit reports if you are going to benefit from a search of the Company Register.

COMPANY INFORMATION

Company name: Telephone:

Address:

Company Size in terms of:
Capital employed
Turnover
Number of employees

Parent/Subsidiaries/
Associated Companies

Products or services

Location of major
plants/branches

Company literature
eg. Annual Report?

Do you know anyone who works
or has worked there?

Reputation

Growth prospects

A good starting point is the company's last annual report. It will give you most of the information you would find from a company search, but in a more digestible and readable form. It will also include details of the various subsidiary companies, if any, and brief information about their products or services. You should have no problem in getting the report—simply telephone the company concerned.

In addition to the annual report some companies issue catalogues containing detailed information about their product range, as well as other promotional literature about individual items.

On page 132 there is a form which you may want to draw up and have some photocopies made. It will provide you with a check-list and somewhere to enter the information you will need about most of the companies in which you are interested.

For general company information there are all kinds of business directories available in most public libraries. A word of caution, though. It must always be remembered that the information contained in a directory can be anything up to two or even three years out of date. It takes about a year to gather or update the information in a major directory. By the time it is printed and distributed and appears on the library shelf, some of the information will already be 12–15 months or so out of date. So never rely on the directory for the names of company personnel. If it is important for you to know the name of the managing director or the personnel manager of a company, for example, you will have to make a telephone call to check the name of the person currently holding that position.

Some of the directories you will find on the library business information shelves include:

Kompass (UK)
Crawford's Directory of City Connections
Who owns Whom?
Kelly's Directory
Guide to Key British Enterprises

Stock Exchange Year Book
Moodies or *Extel* Cards

In addition there are directories covering most industries and professions, as well as specialist directories such as the *National Training Index*, the *Personnel Manager's Yearbook* and many others.

Information about growth prospects will be difficult to find in directories—the annual report is more likely to provide clues about future prospects, although they may sometimes paint an optimistically rosy picture. For more independent opinions on information of this kind you will need to talk to a friendly bank manager or accountant or any reliable business contact.

So there is no shortage of information; it is just a matter of knowing where to look for it and making allowances for some of it being several years out of date. It only remains for you to record it in a form which is easy to file and retrieve when you want it.

15 Assessing the Interviewer

In Chapter 5 I said that the interviewer will probably make up his or her mind about you in the first 90 seconds of an interview. Interviewers may well have the luxury of 90 seconds, but you have got to make a similar assessment of them within seconds of meeting them, so that you can judge how to respond to them and their questions.

This is not so difficult as it may appear. Whenever we meet somebody for the first time, whatever the circumstances, we subconsciously form an instant opinion of him or her. It could be at a party, or when we walk into a shop and talk to the sales person, or meet a new business contact. At the time we don't give it a lot of thought. Later on, when describing some-body we've met, we might say: 'I liked him (or her) from the moment I met him—a really friendly person,' or, 'I took an instant dislike to that new manager in the off-licence . . .' or, 'He seemed a bit shady to me—I didn't like him at all—I was with him for all of twenty minutes and he never once looked me in the eye,' or, 'What a charming man—very clever, too!'

If you form an immediate opinion of somebody you meet at a party and you change that opinion later on when you get to know him or her better, nothing is lost—nothing hangs on your first judgement. But when you meet your interviewer for the first time, everything hangs on your consciously assessing him or her correctly, because you have only one chance to develop that much sought-after rapport.

There will be plenty of clues to help you make your assessment.

When you go into his or her office, is there a friendly atmosphere and is he (let's assume it's a 'he', though it could apply equally to a 'she') sitting behind a large desk with a window behind it, and does he ask you to sit opposite him with the bright light in your eyes so that you can barely see him? Or does he get up and welcome you, motion you to a comfortable chair, join you, and ask you whether you would like a coffee? How is he dressed—formally or more relaxed? (These days, fewer and fewer people wear jackets in their office even for one-to-one interviews, although it's still usual to wear a jacket when the chairman or the managing director is present.)

Does he address you as Mr Taylor or by your first name, or maybe he doesn't use a name at all? Is he an aggressively enthusiastic extrovert or quietly laid back? Does he appear to have a sense of humour?

Is his desk neat and tidy with, perhaps, a framed picture of his children on it, and just your file—nothing else? Or is the desk smothered in papers, through which he has to search to find your file?

From these clues you can deduce whether your interviewer is one of the 'old school', intent on giving the impression of being the boss, or a more friendly, understanding person. You will know whether he has an organised mind or is an energetic go-getter. Remember, if you get the job you may have to work with this man or woman.

But also, beware! The formal, more serious person is often easier to respond to. You know where you are and what is expected of you. You can never be quite sure whether the more relaxed person is truly more relaxed or is putting on a smooth, friendly act, because the interviewing course he attended said it was the right way to communicate.

You will need practice to assess your interviewer accurately in those first few seconds and you won't always get it right, but when you do it will help you to give a much more confident 'performance'. Try the revision questions on the next page and see how you would fare so far.

Revision Questions, Chapter 15

1 Why do you need consciously to assess the interviewer?

2 What clues are there to help you with your assessment?

3 How would you interpret these clues?

4 Having made your assessment, what do you have to be wary of?

The model answers are on page 198.

16   The First Eliminating Interviews

When you are applying for a job you will certainly be interviewed once, but in many cases you will be interviewed twice, and occasionally more than twice, especially by larger companies. The interviews will be conducted sometimes by one person and sometimes by a panel of several people.

The first interview will probably be with the personnel manager whose job it is to *eliminate* applicants, so that four or five candidates can be short-listed, and go forward to a final *decision-making* interview.

The final interview will usually be conducted by the department head or the director whose vacancy it is—the person who can say 'yes' or 'no' to your appointment.

For more senior vacancies there could be more than one 'final' interview—first perhaps by the department head and then by the director with overall responsibility for that part of the firm's activities.

At the other end of the scale there may be only one interview, which would be decision-making. Quite often this will be conducted by more than one person—perhaps the personnel manager who is in effect an eliminator, and the director whose vacancy it is and who is the decision-maker. In this event you need to combine the first and final interview techniques. I shall come back to that shortly.

Sometimes an interview will be conducted by a panel of several people. This is often the case for government posts and for charitable or other institutions. The panel interview is amongst the most unnerving and is especially difficult when it is final and decision-making. It is hard to establish a rapport with a panel, which is essential in order to get a true impression of the company and the people you will be working with if the job is offered to you and you accept it.

It is important that you find out how many interviews there will be *before* you attend the first one. It is usually just a matter of telephoning the secretary of the person who has written to you. If the secretary does not know the answer, don't be put off. Explain that you need to know the number of interviews so that you can prepare for them properly, and that you would appreciate it if she could find out for you.

The reason you want this information is that, as we shall see shortly, you will handle the final interview quite differently from the eliminating ones. Your objectives are different. At the earlier interviews it is to stay on the short-list and move on to the next stage. At the final interview your objective is to get to the top of the short-list and be offered the job.

In this chapter and the next one I shall assume that there are two interviews for the Eastling Enterprises job. The first, eliminating interview will be conducted by the personnel manager and the final, decision-making one by a panel of three.

We are now going to eavesdrop on an interview conducted by the personnel manager of Eastling Enterprises whose advertisement for the vacancy appears on page 112. Her name is Jayne Wilson.

John Taylor is the applicant whose CV and letter of application we have already studied and which appear on pages 82 and 118 respectively.

However, the first interviewee for the job is called Richard. For the purposes of this exercise, he has the same CV as John

Taylor, but he has not had the benefit of training in interview techniques. Let's join the interview now. Jayne Wilson is giving Richard some background to the company:

JAYNE WILSON: Since we were taken over last November by ABC Distribution we've developed our range of products extensively, and although we distribute nationally we've centralised our buying and despatch activities at Herne Bay. Before that they were located in four different locations.

Jayne hesitates for a moment to give Richard the opportunity to comment or ask a question, but he says nothing.

JAYNE: So, you were made redundant in your last job?

Richard considers this a statement rather than a question and still says nothing.

JAYNE: What happened?

RICHARD: Well, my department was combined with another department and the manager of the other department was senior to me so he stayed and I went.

Richard doesn't waste words.

JAYNE: I see from your CV that you were responsible for buying electrical components—so what interests you in the job at Eastling Enterprises?

RICHARD: Well, first of all I need a job and I thought with my buying experience I could easily do the job you're advertising. After all, buying is buying. I don't think it makes much difference what you are buying—it could be switches or paper fasteners; it all comes down to the same thing in the end—getting the best price from your suppliers.

JAYNE: Um . . . tell me, Richard, what are your plans for the future—where do you see yourself in five years' time?

RICHARD: Still working, I hope! No, seriously, I want to progress and be sure of a good future.

JAYNE: Suppose you were faced with this situation, what would you do? One of our Local Authority customers has ordered . . .

Jayne continues with the interview by putting a 'crisis' situation to Richard and asking for his comments . . . but by now she will have decided whether or not she will eliminate Richard. If you had been interviewing Richard, would you have come to a decision so quickly?

Read through that short dialogue between Jayne and Richard again. Jot down your comments on Richard's performance and whether you would have responded differently. Then read on and compare your comments with mine.

*   *   *

I have said that it will take an experienced interviewer not more than 90 seconds to decide whether or not to eliminate an interviewee. Jayne had decided to eliminate Richard in little over a minute, because clearly Richard had not planned for the interview and had no idea how to respond to her.

The decision is largely instinctive, but it is based on the initial visual impression of the applicant, body language during the interview, and whether a dialogue can be developed to which the interviewee is contributing. It is not just a matter of asking a series of questions and getting answers. Jayne gave Richard two opportunities to contribute, but he ignored both of them. But more about that later on.

The first step towards a successful interview is preparation, so let's talk about that now and then I shall analyse Richard's interview in more detail. Preparation is so important that you may want to make some notes to which you can refer when preparing for your own interviews.

PREPARING FOR AN INTERVIEW

The starting point is the letter (or telephone call) you will receive, inviting you to attend an interview.

It will contain two important bits of information—where and when. The place may not necessarily be the same as at the top of the letter.

If you already have another appointment at the time you've been asked to attend, telephone the secretary of the person who has written to you, explain the position and arrange an alternative—there will seldom be any difficulty. Always write and confirm your acceptance, restating the date and time to make sure there is no doubt.

You now need to set up a separate file for this company, starting with the advertisement and your letter of application.

You will need to make two lists: List A will include the points which you expect the interviewer to raise and List B will include the points which you yourself wish to raise. Go through List A and decide how you will respond to the questions you expect. Don't over-rehearse your replies, because you may not get the question or it may not be in precisely the same form as you are expecting.

Then you have three pieces of research to do. The first is the place of the interview.

You need to know exactly where it is and, if practicable, do a dummy run to find out how long it will take you to get there. You will need to arrive at the interview at least ten minutes early. If you arrive exactly on time you will have been tensed up for fifteen minutes before you get there for fear that you are going to be late—no way to start an interview.

The second piece of research is about the company.

There is a lot of information you will need about the company if you are going to commit your next career to it. In Chapter 14 we discussed the sources of company information and how to find them. You will need to complete one of the company information forms (see page 132) which you can file with the advertisement and your letter of application for this vacancy.

You may not have time to get all the information for the first interview, but you will certainly need it for a second interview if there is one.

The third piece of research is yourself.

Turn up the forms you completed for the Real You in Chapter 6, especially your job successes and failures, and draw out as much information as you can which is relevant to the job for which you are going to be interviewed. Pick out your achievements—they are just what you want for those silences which happen during interviews or when the interviewer asks whether there is anything else you want to say.

So you are on the way to your first interview. Take your file with you and arrive ten minutes early. This will ensure that you arrive relaxed and it will give you time to check through the file and remind yourself of the facts you have discovered about the company and any points you wish to raise.

It will also give you time to have a brief chat with the personnel manager's secretary—more often than not you will be waiting in the secretary's office which may adjoin the personnel manager's office. You'd be surprised what you can learn from these chats, but much more important than that, you are making yourself known to the secretary, so that when the personnel manager comes out of his or her office at the end of the day and says to the secretary: 'Phew . . . I'm glad that's over, what did you think of that lot? Who would you have chosen? What about the one who came in just after lunch . . . ?' she may well have something good to say about you.

At the same time you can check how to pronounce the interviewer's name and, if she is female, whether she likes to be called Miss, Mrs, or Ms.

So, the moment of truth. The secretary says: 'Mrs Wilson will see you now, this way please.'

And Mrs Wilson, who is an experienced interviewer, is going

to make up her mind about you instinctively within the first 90 seconds—maybe before you have even sat down.

I remember interviewing for a new receptionist for an advertising agency I was running some years ago. One girl after another came into my office—and then one came in who was the obvious choice as soon as she walked through the door. It was a right choice, too, and she stayed with us for the next five years—until she got married.

So that initial impression is important. Your clothes, for instance—is your suit well pressed or your dress neat and tidy? Did you pop into the loo to check that your hair is combed or your make-up looks good? Are you entering the room confidently? Have you thanked the secretary for showing you in? Have you addressed the interviewer by his or her name: 'Good afternoon, Mrs Wilson'? And, of course, have you given an impression of being relaxed, yet lively? This can come only with the confidence gained from interview experience.

Experienced interviewers will want to put you at your ease, and if they are seated behind a grand desk they will probably emerge from it, usher you to a comfortable chair and join you.

RICHARD'S INTERVIEW—AN ANALYSIS

Now, with your notes and your first appraisal of Richard's interview in front of you, let's analyse it in detail.

We do not know what *visual* impression he gave to the interviewer when he entered the room but, judging by his *verbal* performance during the interview, we can probably guess that the initial impression could have been improved.

Jayne Wilson was giving Richard a little of the background about the Company and continued:

'Since we were taken over last November by ABC Distribution we've developed our range of products extensively, and although we distribute nationally, we've centralised our buying and despatch activities at Herne Bay . . .'

She hesitated briefly at this point to give Richard the chance to make a comment if he wanted to. He didn't.

'So you were made redundant in your last job?'

This was in fact a question, although Richard did not recognise it as such. He probably acknowledged it with a nod of the head, but missed the opportunity of putting his side of the story and developing a conversation with the interviewer, until Jayne asked:

'What happened?'

Richard had no option but to reply now:

'Well, my department was combined with another depart-ment and the manager of the other department was senior to me so he stayed and I went.'

The answer was concise and stated the facts, but we can almost hear the tone of voice in which he spoke the words—resigned, dispirited, as though he had a permanent chip on his shoulder because life had been so unkind to him. It is not just a matter of *what* you say, it's *how* you say it that is just as important. You couldn't speak the words that Richard used without their sounding resigned and almost contemptuous of the question.

Instead he should have explained what these two depart-ments were, the reason why they were combined, and then finish the sentence on the lines of: '. . . and although my col-league David Henshaw and I were doing similar jobs, he'd been with the firm about five years longer than I had. One of us had to go—unfortunately it was me—one of those things.'

Incidentally it is worth noting that whatever reason you are giving for leaving a firm, never criticise your previous employers. Even if you have had a flaming row with them and in your view they sacked you unreasonably—don't criticise them. Whatever the truth of the matter, it will be a mark against you with the interviewer.

JAYNE: I see from your CV that you were responsible for buying electrical components—so what interests you in the job at Eastling Enterprises?

RICHARD: Well, first of all I need a job and I thought with my buying experience I could easily do the job you're advertising. After all, buying is buying. I don't think it makes much difference what you are buying—it could be switches or paper fasteners; it all comes down to the same thing in the end—getting the best price from your suppliers.

Richard should have said *why* he thinks he could do the job and *how* he could contribute to the company. It was his opportunity to start selling himself. Something on these lines: '. . . as I understand it, you sell a very wide range of products, much of it by mail order, and profit margins on individual items are probably tight—that's exactly what I've been used to. I had a range of 3,000 items to buy and keep track of in my last job and keeping costs to a minimum was my main concern.'

That answer would have shown that he understood what the new job was likely to entail and that he had got the right experience to do it.

JAYNE: Tell me, Richard, what are your plans for the future— where do you see yourself in five years' time?

RICHARD: Still working, I hope! No, seriously, I want to progress and be sure of a good future.

You will remember I said that you needed to make two lists— the points you expect the interviewer to raise and the points you wish to raise yourself. Richard had done neither of these things, so he wasn't prepared for the questions and he wasn't prepared with his answers.

Amongst more interviewers' questions there are six favourites:

1 Why are you leaving your present job?
2 Why are you interested in this job?

3   How do you see your future career developing?
4   How would you deal with this crisis?
5   Are you willing to move?
6   What salary are you looking for?

I have already suggested how Richard should have dealt with the reason why he left his last job and why he was interested in the job for which he was being interviewed.

In the planning of your campaign you will, of course, have given thought to your long-term future and indeed should have an idea of what you hope to be doing in five years' time.

With your knowledge of the company through your research, you should be able to relate your aims to what you know would be possible within the company. You may have discovered that they are opening up branches in Europe, for example, and if you would like to work abroad that's something you could say in your reply. Show that you are ambitious, not just for you, but also for contributing to the company's future expansion plans.

This is a good time to mention any additional personal effort you might be making to fit yourself better for the job—you may be going for some additional qualifications, for example. Now is the time to say so.

Although Jayne had almost certainly decided to eliminate Richard at an early stage of the interview, she continued with her questions and asked Richard how he would deal with an imaginary crisis situation. You can't plan for a question like this because you don't know what it will be—the best advice is for you to give yourself a few seconds' thinking time to work out a reasoned answer. What the interviewer is looking for is not so much how you would deal with the crisis but what effect the question has on you.

The location of this company is at Herne Bay and you live in Oxbridge (an imaginary town somewhere between Oxford and Cambridge). You are bound to get a question about moving so you must have your answer ready.

The question of salary is a difficult one to deal with—particularly in this case where the advertisement says the salary is negotiable. If you are asked what salary you have in mind you have to be careful in your reply. If you pitch it too high this could eliminate you, and if you pitch it too low the interviewer may think that if that's how you rate yourself you won't be up to the job.

You need to have done some homework and be aware of the salaries being offered for the kind of job you are looking for, so that you have a salary bracket in mind. Or you can throw the question back and ask the interviewer what the company has in mind. If it's thrown back at you again, the interviewer is probably trying to buy you cheaply and you should be wary.

If salary is not mentioned at this interview don't bring it up yourself—wait until the next interview. If what you had in mind was a little on the high side for this company you will be giving the interviewer an excellent opportunity to eliminate you—which, at this interview, is her job.

Finally, the interviewer will probably ask you whether you have anything further to add. Be well prepared for this question and bring out a plum selling point about you, which will convince the interviewer that you are a number one choice and must be included on the short-list.

Here now is that same interview again, but this time Jayne is interviewing John Taylor who has done his homework thoroughly and is well prepared for the interview.

THE JAYNE/JOHN TAYLOR INTERVIEW

JAYNE: Since we were taken over last November by ABC Distribution we've developed our range of products extensively, and although we distribute nationally we've centralised our buying and despatch activities at Herne Bay. Before that they were located in four different locations.

JOHN: If you distribute nationally, why are you based in the South-East?

JAYNE: Well, most of our business is done through mail order and it doesn't really matter where we're based. One of ABC's warehouses was based in Herne Bay and was exactly right for our operation. So you were made redundant from your last job?

JOHN: Yes, it really was a disappointment because I was thoroughly enjoying the job. I was responsible for buying electrical components and my colleague, David Henshaw, was responsible for buying electrical engineering supplies. A turn-down in business meant rationalisation and our two departments were combined. David had been with the firm longer than I and one of us had to go—it was me. One of those things.

JAYNE: What interests you in the job here at Eastling Enterprises?

JOHN: As I understand it, you sell a very wide range of products and I would imagine that your sales costs are high—especially with that coloured catalogue you produce—so buying costs need to be kept as low as possible, all the same problems which I was coping with at Oxford Motors. I was responsible for buying a wide range of items and my performance was continuously assessed by monthly stock levels and costs. It seems to me that's exactly what I'd be doing for you. All I'd need to learn is the range and to get to know the suppliers.

JAYNE: Tell me, John, what are your plans for the future—where do you see yourself in five years' time?

JOHN: I read the other day that ABC Distribution is expanding into Europe and I would very much like to work abroad for a time—so that's one ambition. Otherwise I would hope to progress with the company in whatever area I can contribute best.

JAYNE: How good are you in a crisis? Suppose one of our Local Authority clients had ordered half a million envelopes for the despatch of election notices. You've ordered them from your regular supplier but they haven't arrived and you can't supply the customer from stock—so you ring up the supplier only to discover that they have a strike on their hands and can't promise when they'll deliver. You can't reach your boss so you've got to make a decision—what would you do?

JOHN (*pause for thought*): . . . Well, I'd certainly contact the customer and explain the situation and ask whether they could give us a bit of time—the chances are they wouldn't be able to if they've an election dead-line to meet. So I'd hunt around for an alternative supplier, and even if that meant buying at a higher price we'd have to do so—all that would matter would be getting the envelopes to a major customer like this one on time, whatever the cost.

JAYNE: I see you live in Oxbridge. If you take this job you'd be based at Herne Bay. What would you do about that?

JOHN: I'd move. No way could I travel from Oxbridge to Herne Bay every day. I've already discussed that problem with my wife and we've agreed that maybe I'd have to commute on a weekly basis until we'd found somewhere to live, but of course we'd move.

JAYNE: What salary are you looking for, John?

JOHN: What is the company offering?

JAYNE: Between £15,000 and £18,000.

JOHN: In my last job I was earning £18,000 plus various bonuses so I would hope not to drop much below that, but I'm sure this is something we can discuss.

JAYNE: Have you got any more questions?

JOHN: Yes. Is this a new vacancy or shall I be replacing some-body else?

JAYNE: You'll be taking over from someone else.

JOHN: Why is he leaving?

JAYNE: He's retiring.

JOHN: Is it possible for me to see your buying department before I go? I find it so much easier to think about a job when I've seen where I'd be working.

JAYNE: Yes, of course. Before you go I'll take you round the offices.

John handled that interview quite well. His question about the vacancy showed his genuine interest in the job: it makes a great deal of difference how you handle a new job if you are taking over from somebody else or if it's a new appointment—especi-ally if your predecessor was highly thought of. It was also a perfectly legitimate question for him to ask to see where he would be working.

Remember that an interview is a two-way affair—the inter-viewer is summing you up and you are summing up the com-pany. You are on equal terms. You are not there to be given the third degree. Unless there is a common respect between you and the interviewer, you are unlikely to get on the short-list.

There is little doubt that John's performance *will* earn him a place on the short-list. He will not be eliminated.

*   *   *

Immediately after the interview, before you go home, take yourself to a quiet spot—like the corner table of a nearby café—and go through the interview critically. Note down the questions you were asked and add the new ones to your list of typical interviewer's questions, and note your answers—especially the very much better answers that will now occur to you. Analyse every interview you attend in this way and you will find that your performance at each subsequent interview will improve. It's all part of becoming a professional interviewee and getting to where you want to be—at the top of the list for the job you really want.

This has been a long chapter and it is packed with information. I suggest you leave the whole book alone until tomorrow and then read this chapter through again—you will be surprised how many new points you will pick up the second time round. You may then want to answer the questions on the next page to see how much of the chapter you have retained.

Revision Questions, Chapter 16

1   What are the most important points to note in the letter inviting you to an interview? If the date or time conflicts with another interview, what should you do? Is there any further information you need at this stage? Is there any further action you should take?

2   After receiving the letter inviting you to attend an interview you should make two lists. What are they and what will they include?

3   There are three pieces of research to do now. One of them is about you—taking relevant information from the charts you have prepared. What are the other two? Give examples.

4   Give at least six sources of information for your company research.

5   Arrive at least ten minutes early for your interview. Give three reasons why.

6   The job of the first interviewer is to eliminate and this usually happens in the first 90 seconds of the interview. List some of the factors that can influence an interviewer in your favour during those first 90 seconds.

7   List the six favourite questions of most interviewers. Discuss how you will deal with each one of them.

8 List some of your job successes which you could raise at interview.

9 The question of salary often poses problems at a first interview. What will you say if, 1) the interviewer asks you what salary you want, and 2) the interviewer doesn't mention salary at all?

10 What will you do immediately after the interview?

The model answers to these questions are on page 200.

17 The Final Interview

Your sole aim at the final interview is the job itself. There will probably be very little to choose between you and the other candidates at this stage, and much will depend on the rapport between you and the decision-maker. The personality 'chemistry' must be compatible, otherwise a long-term working relationship will never be established.

The main difference between your handling of this interview and the previous ones is that, apart from selling yourself, you will be asking many more questions about the job and the part you will be playing. You will also be establishing your impressions of the company and the people you have met. It is your last chance to determine whether you want to work for the company if you are offered the job.

If there is only one interview for the job it will, of course, be decision-making and follow the lines of this final interview. However, all the advice given in Chapter 16 is applicable and should be read in conjunction with the advice given in this chapter.

Preparation for the final interview follows similar lines to the previous ones.

The letter will tell you where and when the interview will take place. Take care, because it may not be at the same address as the last one. If it is at a different address, check how long it will take you to get there and do another dummy run if this is possible. Write and confirm that you will attend, restating the time and date.

Next you must prepare three lists. Lists A and B will be as for the first eliminating interviews—the questions which you think the interviewer will ask and the questions you will want to ask about your day-to-day working arrangements. List C will be not so much about facts, as about impressions of the company and the people you have met (see John Taylor's Lists A, B and C below).

As a result of the previous interview you may have discovered that there are gaps in your information about the company. Remedy these now, because at this final interview you will need to be even better informed than you were last time. Use your company information form and update the entries on it in the light of your last interview and the new information you have now discovered.

You have already done the research on yourself and used it last time. However, now that you know more about the company, you may want to change the emphasis when talking about your experience so that it matches the company's needs more closely.

JOHN TAYLOR'S FINAL INTERVIEW

In the last chapter we heard how Richard and John Taylor performed at their first interview. Richard was eliminated as expected, but John has been invited to this final interview. The last interview was at Eastling Enterprises at Herne Bay, but this one is at the headquarters of the ABC Group in London. He has checked the location and how long it will take him to get there.

He arrives in good time and discovers from the secretary that there will be three interviewers: David Banks, who is

Purchasing Director for the ABC Group; Jayne Wilson, who is the Group Personnel Manager and who interviewed him last time; and Tony Brookes, who is Works Manager at Herne Bay and will presumably be John's immediate boss if he gets the job. He makes a mental note to check whether this will be so. He also discovers that there are three candidates on the short-list, so he has two rivals. He hasn't been able to find out anything about them, although he has tried.

Since the last interview John has been preparing for this one. In his Eastling Enterprises file he now has the following documents:

> The original advertisement (see page 112).
> His letter of application (see page 118).
> A copy of his CV (see pages 82 and 83).
> The updated company information form (see page 132).
> His notes on the last interview (see below).
> List A—the questions he thinks he will be asked (see below).
> List B—the questions he wishes to raise (see below).
> List C—the questions he must ask himself about his impressions of the company (see below).

He also has a copy of the ABC Group annual report and the Eastling Enterprises mail order catalogue.

Although he will have the file with him, he will not use it at the interview. He will have committed the lists to memory and can remind himself of them on the way to the appointment.

Here are the *notes he made immediately after the last interview*:

> I should have asked more about the purchasing department at Herne Bay—how many staff and so on.
>
> I could have said more about my future aims and how I thought I could contribute to the firm's prosperity.
>
> I didn't get any reaction when I said I would like to work abroad.

I'm concerned about the salary they have in mind—it's too low.

I should have asked about other companies in the group.

No reaction to my crisis solution but I think it was OK.

I wonder what sort of person I would be taking over from. I hoped I would meet him when I went round the offices.

Seemed like a good atmosphere in the place—people were actually smiling!

Here is his *List A*—the questions he thinks he will be asked:

Why are you leaving your job?
What interests you in this job?
What are your future career plans?
How would you deal with this crisis?
Are you willing to move?
What salary are you looking for?

And here is *List B*—the questions he needs to ask at the interview:

What is the chain of responsibility—how many people shall I be responsible to?
Is Head Office involved in day-to-day decisions?
What budget shall I be responsible for?
How many people in my department?
How long has the person I would be taking over from been with the company?
To what extent is the buying department computerised?
What are the working hours?
What pension arrangements are there?
What is the holiday entitlement?

(The question about the number of bosses an applicant will be working for is particularly important if you are applying for a secretarial or personal assistant appointment.)

Here is John's new *List C*—the questions he wants to ask

himself about his impressions of the company before he accepts
the job, if he is offered it:

> About the person he will be responsible to:
>> Could I work with this person?
>> Are we on the same wavelength?
>> Will the 'chemistry' be right?
>> Has he a sense of humour?
> About the working environment:
>> Is the working atmosphere good?
>> Do I want to work in Kent?
>> Shall I be free to make decisions?

As in the earlier interviews, the first 90 seconds are vital, but
in fact your interview starts from the moment you enter the
room and before a word is spoken. In the case of John Taylor,
three pairs of eyes will be focused on him as soon as the door
opens, and three interviewers will be making an instant assessment of him. So his appearance and his courtesy in thanking
the secretary who showed him in will influence that immediate
impression. And remember: it may take the interviewers 90
seconds to make up their minds about you, but you have even
less time to assess them and decide how you will respond to
their questions.

So how will John Taylor come through his final interview?
Let's follow him through that door and see how well he
performs.

*   *   *

Purchasing Director David Banks' office was a large airy one,
sparsely furnished, with a desk in one corner and a separate
rectangular table in the middle of the room. The desk had little
but a bank of telephones on it. He was a benevolent-looking
gentleman nearing retirement age and was seated at one end
of the table. Jayne Wilson, whom John had met at his last
interview, was seated at the right hand side of the table, and

on the opposite side was the third interviewer, presumably Tony Brookes.

David Banks rose to greet him.

'Good afternoon, Mr Taylor,' he said. 'Thank you very much for coming to see us, please take a seat.'

John walked forward and shook hands with Mr Banks before taking the only other seat which was placed at the end of the table opposite David Banks who then introduced Jayne Wilson and Tony Brookes, 'our Works Manager at Eastling Enterprises'. They each had a note pad in front of them and a folder, which contained copies of John's CV, letter of application and a report of his last interview by Jayne Wilson.

Tony Brookes was in his late forties, with a set, unsmiling expression on his face. He could be ruthless, thought John, who was beginning to feel uneasy about this interview.

'Can I offer you a coffee or tea?' asked David Banks.

'Thank you very much,' replied John, 'but I'd prefer a glass of water or mineral water if that's convenient.'

He had remembered that when one's mouth is going dry because of nerves, water is a much more effective lubricant than coffee. His unease probably had nothing to do with Mr Brookes' unsmiling face; it was much more likely to be the unfamiliar situation of being interviewed by three people—it was his first experience of it. In this case it was aggravated by the seating arrangement. When John was speaking to one of the interviewers he couldn't see the reaction, if any, of the others. It would have been easier if he had been on one side of the table and the three interrogators on the other side. Most thoughtful interviewers would arrange it that way because they gain nothing by making things unnecessarily difficult for the interviewee. However, there was nothing John could do to change that.

David Banks raised his eyes from the papers in front of him.

'I have read Jayne Wilson's report of your interview with her,' he said, 'but I wonder whether you could expand a little on what interests you in the job at Eastling Enterprises.'

It is a favourite ploy of interviewers to ask you the same question you were asked in a previous interview, knowing full well what you said last time. They are checking on the consistency of your answer. They want to know whether you were 'bending the truth' and have forgotten what you said. This illustrates the importance of making notes immediately after an interview so that you can remind yourself of how you replied to questions before you are interviewed by the same company again.

John gave a similar reply to last time except that he added: '. . . and now that I've seen your operation at Herne Bay, I am more convinced than ever of the similarities between what you do there and what I have been used to.'

Tony Brookes then asked a question:

'I see from your CV that in your last job you had a staff of ten people which included eight clerical assistants—that seems a lot of people for a stock level of £2.75 million.'

John had not expected that one and thought for a second or two before he replied.

'When I left the Oxford Motor Company we were in the last phase of updating our computer systems and installing a fully automated stock control system with the bar-coding of each product line. In fact, I think the installation of the new system made it easier for the company to combine the two buying departments and probably contributed to my redundancy. Would I be right in supposing you have a fully integrated stock control system at Herne Bay?

'Yes, you would. If you were only installing a system at Oxford Motor Company, am I to gather you have very little experience of computerised stock control?'

'On the contrary. We always have had a computerised system and from the start I was involved in the design of the much more sophisticated system which was coming on stream when I left.'

When preparing for the interview John should have realised that a question on his management of the buying department at the Oxford Motor Company was bound to arise. It should not have taken him by surprise. As it turned out, his answer was perfectly satisfactory and he had managed to emphasise his experience of computerised stock control systems.

Then it was Jayne Wilson's turn:

'When I interviewed you at Herne Bay you said you were interested in working abroad. That doesn't seem to add up with your having one child still at school.'

'Sarah will shortly be leaving school for college, and as both my wife and I love travelling we would be more than willing to work abroad for a while if the opportunity arose.'

'What about languages?'

'I speak some French and I am currently taking a French conversation course. I'm sure that if I lived in the country for only a few months I would very quickly become reasonably fluent in the language.'

Tony Brookes spoke up again:

'We have a smoking ban in the works at Herne Bay—would that be a problem?'

'Not at all—I don't smoke so I would welcome it.'

Suppose you are a smoker—how would you have reacted to the same question? It would be just one more factor in the balance between compatibility, salary and location which you would have to decide upon before accepting the job.

The interview continued on a question and answer basis for another fifteen minutes. John was uneasy about the aggressive nature of Tony Brookes' questioning because this was the man he would be responsible to and have to work with on a day-to-day basis. So when David Banks asked John whether he had any questions, he decided to address them to Tony Brookes.

As I said in the last chapter, an interview is a two-way affair—it's just as important for the interviewer to know that you can do the job and whether you will fit into the company structure as it is for you to know that you will be happy working there. 'Interview' is, perhaps, the wrong word for this final meeting with your prospective employer. It should be a conversation during which you are both finding out as much as you can about each other to ensure that there will be a mutually beneficial working relationship for a long time to come.

Up until now John had been apprehensive about the belligerent attitude that Tony Brookes had adopted throughout the interview. So he tried to develop a more relaxed atmosphere by asking this man about the chain of responsibility and the day-to-day working arrangements, to give himself the opportunity of judging how well they would communicate if they were working together.

Finally, there was the question of his salary. He asked Jayne Wilson whether the company had given any further consideration to his salary since his first interview with her, when the question of salary had been left open. As he thought he would, David Banks took up the question and said that he had noted John's concern about salary in Jayne's report and that if the job was offered to him he thought that the salary would be acceptable. There was no point in John trying to get a more specific answer at that interview.

*   *   *

Eventually the interview will come to an end and you will have made sure that the interviewer is aware of all your experience and skills. Above all, you will have conveyed your enthusiasm for working for the company and for contributing to its expansion. At the same time you will have decided whether your priorities of compatibility, salary and location will be met.

Immediately after the interview, and before you go home, do the same critical self-analysis as you did after the first interview. Until you receive a letter offering you the job and you have accepted it, you haven't got the job—so your job-getting campaign continues unabated. Keep on applying for other jobs— keep on going to interviews. No interview is the last one until you are employed in a new job.

If all goes well you will get a letter in a few days or so offering you the job and this is the subject of the next chapter.

There are some revision questions on this chapter on the next page.

Revision Questions, Chapter 17

1 What is your aim in this final interview? How does that differ from your aim in the previous interviews for the same job?

2 What is the main difference in the way you will perform at a final interview compared with the previous ones?

3 For the first interview you prepared two lists—one for the questions you thought the interviewer would ask, and the other, the questions *you* wanted to ask. There is a third list for this final interview. What is it?

4 Summarise some of the questions you would expect to find in the third list.

5 You will have prepared a file for each company that invites you for interview. It will contain at least six separate items of information. What are they?

6 The question of how many bosses an applicant will be working for is of particular importance for certain appointments. What are they?

7 What do you need to find out before going into the interview? How will you do this?

8 It is a favourite ploy of interviewers at the final interview

to ask you a question which is identical to one asked in an earlier interview. Why?

9   When there is more than one interviewer, to which one should you address your questions about day-to-day working arrangements? Why?

10   What action should you take in your job-getting campaign after the final interview is over?

The model answers to these questions are on page 203.

18   The Contract

The first step towards your new appointment will be a letter making an offer which should contain certain information.

Conditions of employment are laid down in several Acts of Parliament, amongst which the two most important are the Employees Protection (Consolidation) Act 1978, and the Trade Unions Reform and Employment Rights Act 1993.

These Acts lay down what information must be provided by an employer to an employee and when it has to be given. The first offer of a permanent job should contain the following information:

The identity of the employer (in the example we have been studying in this book it will be either Eastling Enterprises or ABC Distribution).
The job title.
The starting date.
The salary and how it is to be paid.
The place or places of work.
The hours of work (for management appointments there will almost certainly be an escape clause here which ensures that you will work whatever hours are necessary to do the job).
Holiday entitlement and holiday pay.

Then, within a period of two months, the employer must provide further information such as:

What notice has to be given by both sides to terminate the employment.

Sickness procedures and sickness pay.

Details of the pension scheme.

Disciplinary procedures.

The employer may not be obliged to put all the information in writing but, instead, may say where the 'rule book' is located and when it can be inspected.

You will be asked to confirm your acceptance of the offer.

Once you have accepted the offer you have also accepted in law all the terms in the letter, so make sure you agree with them. Never rely on any verbal promises at the interview which do not appear or have been varied in the letter. If there is a formal contract to be signed apart from the letter, you can, of course, accept the terms in the letter 'subject to contract', which would refer to the formal document to follow.

You may remember that in Chapter 5 I suggested that your aim is to get offers of more than one job before making a final decision, otherwise you may be tempted to accept the first job offered, but for all the wrong reasons. Clearly, in times of high unemployment it may be difficult to follow this advice, but it can happen.

What do you do, then, when you have been given a time limit for accepting a job—as you always will be—and you are waiting for another offer?

You have only one option: to be frank. Ask the person who has made the offer whether he can spare you a few minutes so that you can put the circumstances before him. He will understand your problem—indeed, he would be surprised if you had not got other irons in the fire. Ask him how long he can wait for an answer to enable you to make the right decision which, after all, will affect you and your family for many years to come.

Generally, he will be amenable. In a way he has got to be, because if he refuses he has got to go back to his short-list, and by now the names on it may have accepted other jobs. He might even have to go back to square one and start advertising all over again. But apart from that, the last thing an employer wants is to take someone on who thinks he could have done better for himself elsewhere.

Incidentally, much as you will want to know whether you are being offered a job after the final interview, avoid the temptation to telephone the company and ask them. It will serve no purpose other than to irritate them. On the other hand, if you were told at the interview that you would hear from the company by such and such a date, it would be perfectly reasonable to wait for a few days after that date and telephone them then. Letters have been known to get lost in the post.

Never use the offer of another job to force a decision. Potential employers don't take kindly to threats and you will gain nothing from it.

If you are required to sign a formal contract, read it through very carefully and make sure you agree to all the terms in it. If in doubt, ask for clarification and, if necessary, take independent advice. Most contracts of employment from reputable companies look more formidable than they are, but it is very important that you have no doubts about your commitment, bearing in mind that the contract could be in force for the rest of your working life.

19 A Summary

At the beginning of this book I said that you had a long and tough campaign ahead. There are many books and courses which set out to give tips and general help on writing CVs, interviewing techniques and getting a job, but it seems to me that very few of them emphasise the need to get into training as an athlete would who wants to win a gold medal at the Olympics.

Think about it for a minute. Take any job that you would dearly like—you would enjoy the work; compatibility would be just right; the salary would be what you need to live comfortably; the location is near your home; and, above all, it offers a career plan which exactly fits into your own future plans.

There are hundreds of people after that job. You have taken the trouble to work through a book like this one and you have understood why you need to get into training for job-getting, a task in which you previously had little or no experience. You do all that and you end up on a short-list of, say, four or five candidates for your ideal job. Only one of you will get it. Only one athlete wins a gold medal in any event. And those who win do so because they are at their peak performance plus. They have slogged round the streets of Fulham or wherever week after week. They have had setbacks and disappointments.

But sheer, dogged determination and self-discipline have eventually got them the gold medal they deserve.

Job-getting is just the same—there is no magic route to the top. It is a lonely game and it will take you three months, six months, nine months, or even longer before you win your gold.

By now you should have every possible selling point about the Real You at your finger-tips. You should have the perfect piece of sales literature—your CV—well printed and widely distributed amongst your friends and acquaintances. You will have set up files on companies you would like to work for and you are reading the business press every day for snippets of information, which could spark off a round-robin from you to a company telling them how you would like to contribute to their operation.

You are applying for jobs in which you are not particularly interested just to get interview experience. In all probability you will already have attended some first interviews and, as a result of your critical self-analysis after each interview, you will be well aware of your strengths and weaknesses.

A final word to those of you who are out of work rather than looking for a job while you are still employed. Some people find that the solitary nature of working alone from home is a serious problem. This would particularly apply to people such as Chris, who live on their own. The Jobclubs, set up by the government for people who have been unemployed for six months or more, provide one solution to this problem. It is well worth discovering whether there is a Jobclub in your district and to join it. Apart from the opportunity to share your problems with others in a similar situation, the Jobclub offers all kinds of practical help such as the use of typewriters, telephones, photocopiers, stationery and so on, as well as advice from the Jobclub leaders.

From time to time during your campaign there will be periods when you appear to be making no progress at all and the temptation to 'give up' is hard to resist. When the pressure becomes unbearable, then is the time to take a week's 'holiday' from the daily routine of visiting the library and applying for interviews. If your budget will allow you to go away for a few days, so much the better. An occasional short break will refresh you and make it easier for you to stick to your routine until you have achieved your objective.

Keep a close watch on your cash flow forecast. Financial problems are one of the most serious worries for people who are unemployed, with no idea how long their reserves have to last. By updating your cash flow forecast every month you will maintain control of your finances, which will give you peace of mind and avoid unpleasant surprises.

I suggest that now and then you read through the revision questions which have appeared at the end of some of the chapters. Quite often they will remind you of a point which you had forgotten and prompt you to reread the relevant chapter.

By now you should be well on your way to your next career. May it start soon and all good wishes for your success in it.

Postscript

No two readers of this book, who have been made redundant, will be faced with precisely the same problems. The advice given is broadly based so that you can adapt it to your own particular circumstances. If everybody who read the book responded to an interviewer in exactly the same way and all interviewers made the same judgements, everybody would get to the top of the short-list and nobody would get the job!

But it doesn't work that way. We are all different and our success in finding the job we want depends on our unique contribution which comes from our personality, our imagination and our determination to succeed.

John, Chris and Sally, whom we met at the beginning of the book, all have different problems and a different approach to finding the solutions. Let's hear from each of them.

JOHN TAYLOR

In a sense I suppose I am the luckiest of the three of us because I have the backing of my family, who have given me magnificent support since I was made redundant. Sheila has now got a job which has given us a feeling of security, and the children have never once made me feel that I have let them down.

On the other hand I wonder whether, in a way, I have been having it too easy, which has occasionally taken the edge off my determination to succeed and given me some wonderful excuses for not always following my daily routine.

It is now three months since I was made redundant. It has been much tougher than I had expected, but once I had set up my 'office' at home and established a rigid daily routine, I found it easier. But after a month or so the rigid routine does become tedious. The worst part has been the repetition of the daily tasks, such as going to the library, especially when no progress is being made. The recommendation to take the day off occasionally is a good one, provided you don't do it too often. My other problem is that I am beginning to quite enjoy working from home, which gives me one more excuse for not putting all my effort into finding another job.

Probably the most important piece of advice in the early chapters was the preparation of the budget and the monthly updating of the cash flow forecast. At least it takes away the nagging worry that the money will suddenly run out or the house will be repossessed.

When I started reading this book I thought it was going to tell me how to write a lot of letters of application for jobs and, by the law of averages, I would eventually get employed again. I had no idea, for instance, that I would meet an eliminator at the first interview and a decision-maker at the final interview— and that I needed to approach both interviews quite differently. I certainly had no idea that getting a job was like winning a gold medal at the Olympics. I now know better.

I've learnt a lot about myself. The Real You chapter highlighted my strengths and weaknesses—it was hard to admit to some of the weaknesses, but that was balanced by discovering strengths I didn't know I had.

I believe my CV now sells me as I want to be sold, but it took time to get it right.

I found the chapter on analysing an advertisement interesting, because it had never occurred to me that there can be more to an advertisement than meets the eye. I am now looking at advertisements much more critically, but I think one has to keep an open mind when analysing them. You can get it wrong! It is a good discipline, though, and it has certainly been useful at interviews. It's made me think much more carefully about my letters of application and matching my experience to what I believe the company is looking for.

It's taken me a while to get used to the idea of applying for jobs I don't want just to get interview experience. It seemed mildly dishonest to me. But now I realise what invaluable training it is. What's more I nearly accepted a job the other day which turned out to be much more interesting than I thought it was going to be. More than that, when you're a bit down there's nothing more ego-lifting than attending an interview—even if you don't want the job!

I've been offered the Eastling Enterprises job, but I haven't accepted it yet. They've given me another week to make up my mind. I'm still wary of Tony Brookes and I'm not at all sure that I shall find him easy to work with. Coupled with that, I am waiting to hear about the result of an interview with an engineering company where I would be doing exactly the same job as I had at the Oxford Motor Company. But the money's not so good as Eastling Enterprises is now offering. I shall probably take the Eastling Enterprises job because it will be more of a challenge and the change of industry would be useful experience.

CHRIS WHITE

This has been the worst period of my life and I am still a long way from getting on top of it.

The suddenness of the redundancy numbed me and I suffered a sort of delayed shock for the first week or two. I signed on at the Job Centre as soon as I could and braced myself to ask for help—it was the first time in my life that I had to admit that I couldn't support myself, and my pride took a hammering.

Money has been my big worry. I realised I had to get a part-time job as quickly as possible, and I did get one—a security job with a local firm. It isn't much of a job after being Apprentice Training Manager at the Oxford Motor Company for so many years, but it has restored my confidence a bit. The best of it is that it's an evening job so I have all day to concentrate on getting a permanent one.

I am getting income support and I have been released from paying the council tax.

I've never been one to keep letters and invoices and things like that—I've never kept accounts in my life and hardly ever checked my bank statements. But I could see the point and with a lot of effort I got a budget out. It probably did more than anything else to spur me on to find a new job when I saw how little money I could spend.

I didn't think too much about the idea of learning to type, so I contacted the girl in the office at the Oxford Motor Company who used to type out the training courses for me, and she said she would help me out with typing my letters. If I don't get a job fairly quickly I may have to do my own typing, but I'll delay that as long as possible.

The worst part of all this is being on my own. I liked the training job I was doing because I was always with people. If I'm still unemployed after six months I shall certainly try to get into the local Jobclub. Apparently they will sometimes take disabled people and ex-offenders without the six-month qualifying period—but I'll have to wait.

I am finding it very difficult indeed to concentrate on the advice given in this book and all the preparatory work. But I am persevering because it does make sense and I can't see myself getting another job unless I learn how to set about it.

I've attended a few interviews, but I realise that I still have a long way to go to become what the book calls a professional interviewee—when I can attend any interview with confidence and always get on the short-list. But I'm determined to get there in the end.

SALLY FRASER

It may seem strange, but after the initial shock of losing my job I suddenly realised that I was being given an opportunity. I had always regretted failing to get any proper training or qualification after leaving school. All my work experience had been self-taught, including the research I was doing in the advertising agency, and now I had the opportunity to stand back and think through where I wanted to go and how I was going to get there.

I read this book straight through in one go, despite the advice to take it slowly. I wanted to get a general idea of what I had to do and then start again from the beginning. However, in the first read through I did slow down when I got to Chapter 2—I have a tidy mind and working out my budget didn't present any problem. Having done so I realised that I had a little time before a crisis situation arose and so I decided that my immediate priority was to get a part-time job which would pay better than the dole money and then I would enrol for an Open University course. I could do the course at the same time as looking for a new permanent job. My flatmate is out at work all day and I have the flat to myself. Fortunately, I don't in the least mind being on my own.

I've got a part-time job at the local supermarket, mostly working at weekends, and now I'm looking forward to settling down to my job-hunting campaign and working through the book step by step at the same time as doing the Open University course.

I have given myself a target of six months for finding a new job, and if that doesn't come off I shall have to think again about the Open University course and concentrate solely on the job-hunting.

MODEL ANSWERS
TO THE
REVISION QUESTIONS

Chapter 2: Your Business Plan

1   Whether you like it or not, you *are* in business on your own. You have only one product to sell and that is YOU. You will be approaching your campaign in exactly the same way as you would if you were selling any other goods or services. You will be searching for prospects, contacting them and making your sales calls.

2   Getting control of your finances is the most important part of your business plan, to ensure you will be able to meet your financial commitments until you are employed again.

3   Certainly you must involve your family. Getting you working again is the prime objective and even if you have never before involved your family in your financial affairs, you must do so now. Getting you working is a team effort.

4   Sign on for unemployment benefit AND find out whether you qualify for any income support or other benefits.

5   You have no idea how long it will take you to find a new job and even if you have received a generous redundancy payment, it will melt away quickly unless you keep strict control of your finances.

6   There is every point in investing it. Even though the income from it will be small, it will focus your attention on reducing your expenditure to the lowest possible level. It will also give you peace of mind that you have some

capital to fall back on for emergencies if things go badly wrong for you.

7   a) Your budget and b) your cash flow.

8   If there is a shortfall in your budget your options are: (a) go through your expenditure again and prune it wherever you can; (b) use part of your capital which you have allocated for investment, but this will reduce your income which will increase the shortfall; (c) sell any assets which you can do without (the Taylor family decided to sell their second car).

9   Your expenditure will not be evenly spread throughout the year—you will spend more on heat and light in the winter than in the summer, for example, and some of your expenditure will be once a year or once every quarter. The cash flow will forecast your expenditure each month and show the estimated bank balance at the end of each month.

10   The cash flow forecast shows the *estimated* expenditure. You should update it every month so that it signals problems which may arise later in the year and gives you the opportunity to take the necessary action in advance.

Chapter 3: Working from Home

1   Most people who say 'they couldn't work at home' have
    never tried to do so. It requires a high degree of self-
    discipline which some people believe they will find imposs-
    ible to develop.

2   When we are employed we are obliged to follow a daily
    routine which is imposed on us by our employment. When
    working from home we have to impose that routine on
    ourselves. So the first priority is to establish a working
    regime and stick to it. For example, we need to have a
    set time when we start work each day, just as though we
    were still employed.

3   The other criteria for successful home working are a dedi-
    cated place to work and some house rules. Ideally
    the work area should be a separate room, but if this
    is not practical, at least a separate table or desk should
    be set up in the bedroom, perhaps, and used as an
    'office'.
       The 'house rules' establish that you must be allowed to
    work uninterrupted. It is impossible to work effectively
    and attend to domestic matters at the same time. This is
    particularly important if you are a family person with
    young children.

4   Your basic need is a typewriter so that you can type your
    letters of application and keep copies of them. In addition
    you will need some ring binders, good quality A4 paper
    for your letters, flimsy paper and carbon paper for your

copies. You will also need some ring binders for filing company information and your letters.

5   If you can't type, you will have to learn. It is not at all difficult, and 'one-finger' typing can be quite fast and effective. Sooner or later you will have to operate the keyboard of a personal computer which has the same keyboard as a typewriter, so the sooner you learn the better.

Chapter 4: The Job Market

1   The most important point here is that you are an individual
and you must evolve your own marketing mix to sell yourself. You must talk to other people and listen to what they
say to help you develop your own marketing platform.

2   About 25 per cent.

3   The point that you should have made is that quite often
when a company advertises a vacancy they may not be
looking for somebody to fill the job as advertised—they
may want someone who meets the job specification now,
but who also has the potential to develop with the job as it
expands and can contribute to the company's profitability.

4   Advertising is very expensive. There are often several jobs
to fill at one time with similar job specifications, so one
advertisement can be drafted to meet all the job specifications, thus reducing costs.

5   There are four main reasons. The first is that they may be
checking the current market rate for their own particular
job. Secondly, they may be a plant for their company
wanting information about the competition. Thirdly, they
may be making a business of going to interviews and living
off the expenses they are paid for attending. And fourthly,
domestic pressure may affect their seriousness about
changing their job.

6   Most vacancies are filled by personal contact (the network)

or by being 'passed on' from one personnel manager to another.

7   The most important factors you must consider are: one—compatibility; two—salary; and three—location.

8   Your choice! The question has been included to ensure you analyse the factors which are really important to you—an essential part of the campaign on which you are now embarking.

9   Here are just some of the points made in this chapter:
    a   Talk to as many people as you can to help develop your own marketing mix.
    b   Job specifications for a vacancy seldom fully describe the job to be filled.
    c   At least 75 per cent of vacancies are never advertised.
    d   Many broadly based advertisements refer to more than one vacancy.
    e   Many people apply for a vacancy who are not really serious about changing jobs.
    f   There are three factors you must consider when changing your job: compatibility, salary and location.
    g   An essential part of your campaign is to put these factors into an order of importance to you, because they won't all turn up trumps every time.

Chapter 5: Getting Into Training

1 a On average it will take a man or a woman who has conscientiously worked through this book anything from three to nine months to get a job.
   b You will have written from 150 to 250 letters of application.

2 The three criteria are: compatibility, salary and location.

3 If you take the first job you are offered without considering your criteria, you are likely to fail. The reason is that you have probably accepted the job for the wrong reasons. However, the next question will amplify this point.

4 Yes, provided the salary is right.
   If you are looking for a job worth, say, £20,000 per year, you don't take a job paying £17,000, because once you are in a job paying £17,000 it will be very difficult indeed for you to get back to £20,000. But there is nothing wrong in accepting a job at the right salary, even if it is not the job you really want, while you continue to look for an alternative. You will then be job-searching from strength.

5 The ten words are: 'the time it takes me to become a professional interviewee'.

6 Of course you must ask your friends—that's what friends are for when you are in trouble. You set about it by

making personal contact with them and sending them copies of your CV.

7   Get into conversation with people whenever you can—when travelling by train, for example, or, if you can afford to take a holiday, this will provide an excellent opportunity to meet people in a relaxed and friendly environment.

8   You study the newspapers and trade journals and apply for interviews, even for jobs you don't want, just to get interview experience and to practise assessing your interviewer within the first few seconds, so that you know how to respond.

9   You should be pleased. As a rule, people who claim not to suffer from nerves are either lying or are so insensitive that they will be incapable of giving a good performance at interview.

10 The first step you must take is to determine how nerves affect you—dry mouth, shaking hands, or whatever. Then you must decide how best to overcome your particular problem and put your solution into practice whenever you are interviewed. The more interviews you attend the more your self-confidence will grow and the less you will be affected by nerves.

Chapter 8: Producing Your CV

1   You should get it criticised by as many people as possible.

2   Your critics may remind you of something important which you have omitted. Analyse the criticisms carefully: they may not all be relevant—some of them may have been given by someone who feels he must say something, even though he has nothing to criticise.

3   Preferably a professionally taken photograph, although not necessarily a head and shoulders. A photograph in a more relaxed situation will show you to better advantage. The photo-booth passport-type photograph will NOT do.

4   No. There is always a danger that the wrong CV will be sent when replying to an advertisement, and producing more than one will increase your printing costs. Your CV should be broadly based, suitable for all occasions.

5   Your CV can be typewritten on not more than two pages, using an electronic typewriter or word processor and printed on good quality paper; or it can be typeset and printed.

6   The advantage of the typeset version is that it can probably be contained on one page. The disadvantage is that it may appear to have been professionally written. On balance the two-page typewritten version will appear more personal, will certainly cost less, and is preferred.

Chapter 10: How a Vacancy is Filled

1   A vacancy can be created in three ways: a) because it's a
    new appointment in the company; or b) because two pre-
    vious appointments have been amalgamated; or c) because
    the previous incumbent has left the Company or been
    promoted.

2   The first is the job specification; and the second is the
    personal specification.

3   The job specification is prepared by the department head
    or director who wants the vacancy filled. The personal
    specification is prepared by the personnel manager.

    The job specification defines whom the candidate is
    responsible to, and for what.

    The personal specification includes the experience,
    qualifications and age range of the successful candidate,
    and will usually state the salary.

4   An experienced member of the personnel department with
    an intimate knowledge of the various departments of the
    company first prepares a check-list based on the job speci-
    fication, the personal specification and the advertisement.

    The readers of the letters will then reject those appli-
    cants who are clearly unsuitable. They are the *eliminators*.

5   The applications are then marked out of ten and sorted
    into three trays labelled Rejects, Possibles and Probables,
    based on the check-list and the judgement of the reader.

6 The main reason for rejecting a letter of application is that it is difficult to read or fails to give positive reasons why the applicant should be considered.

Examples are: 'I have read with interest your advertisement and I am confident that I can do the job to our mutual satisfaction'. No positive reason has been given to support that statement.

'I have read etc. . . . . please see my CV attached'. The reader of the letter will not have time to read the CV. It is up to the applicant to give reasons why he or she should be considered for the job.

7 The 'lunatic fringe' are the applicants who would clearly be out of their depth in the job for which they are applying—outside their salary range, for example, and applicants who write a totally unacceptable letter of application.

8 Once the letters have been sorted, the Probables are passed on to the personnel manager who decides whether or not to invite each applicant to complete an application form. The personnel manager may read through the Possibles if there is only a small number of Probables, or if he or she wants to check on the judgement of the eliminators.

9 The same routine will be followed, perhaps by the secretary of the director or manager whose vacancy it is.

10 The missing words are 'eliminate you'.

Chapter 13: Other Self-Marketing Techniques

1   The network is how most job vacancies are filled—your
    network of friends and acquaintances. Make a list of them
    and write a personal note to every one of them with a
    couple of copies of your CV.

2   Round-robins are letters from you to companies you
    would like to work for. By reading the *Financial Times*
    and the business pages of the daily press you will find
    company news which can give you a reason for writing to
    a company and offering your services. You will, of course,
    also have to do some research into the company (Chapter
    14) so that you know something about them.

3   The employment agencies advertise in the job vacancies
    columns of the press, and you will find agencies local to
    you in the *Yellow Pages*. There is also a directory called
    the *Personnel Manager's Yearbook* which should be avail-
    able in your local library and contains the names and
    addresses of hundreds of recruitment agencies throughout
    the country.

4   You need to know how many interviews there are likely
    to be with the company before a decision is made because,
    as we shall see in Chapters 16 and 17, you will respond to
    the first and final interviews differently.

5   You need to know its terms. It should be receiving its
    income from the employer, but some charge both the
    employer and the employee for their services, so make

sure you know in what way you are liable before committing yourself.

6 Yes. Always carry copies of your CV with you. You never know when you may meet someone—on a train perhaps, or in the local pub—and when the conversation turns to 'what do you do?' that is your opportunity to hand over a CV.

Chapter 15: Assessing the Interviewers

1   You need to assess the interviewer so that you know how to respond and reply to questions.

2   Some of the clues to help you with your assessment are: What is your immediate impression of the office? How does the interviewer greet you when you enter the room? Where does he seat you for the interview? What is the state of his desk? How is he dressed? How does he address you? Does he appear to be an introvert or an extrovert? Has he a sense of humour?

3   A well-decorated, airy office with perhaps a picture or two on the wall will suggest the interviewer is sensitive to his surroundings, which may be reflected in the working environment of his employees.

It will suggest that he is a professional interviewer and it will be much easier to communicate with him if he, 1) gets up and greets you in a friendly way; 2) joins you in a comfortable chair away from his desk; 3) asks you whether you want a coffee.

If the interviewer is not wearing a jacket and addresses you by your first name, he is likely to conduct the interview in a more relaxed and less formal way.

A tidy desk suggests a tidy mind.

It is always easier to communicate with a person who has a sense of humour.

4   The more friendly approach can sometimes be misleading and put you off your guard. So pay special attention to his reaction to your answers to his questions.

Chapter 16: The First Eliminating Interviews

1   The place—which may not be the same as the address at the top of the letter—and the time.

   If the time or date conflicts with another appointment telephone the secretary of the person who has written to you—there will seldom be any difficulty in making an alternative appointment.

   You need to know how many interviews there will be.

   You should write and confirm your acceptance, restating the date and time of the interview.

2   The first list should contain points which you think the interviewer will raise so that you have an outline of your replies thought out in advance. The second list will comprise items you want to ask about the job.

3   The two additional pieces of research are:
   1   To establish the location of the interview—how you are going to get there and how long it will take you—and if possible, to make a dummy run.
   2   To check that you have all the information you want about the company.

4   The company's annual report and promotional literature are two of them. Other sources are included in a list on page 133 in Chapter 14.

5   1   To make sure you arrive in a relaxed state and not tensed up because you were worried about being late.

2   To give you time to glance through your file and refresh your memory before the interview.

3   To talk to the interviewer's secretary who is often an important person in her own right. The interviewer may well ask her opinion of the candidates after the interviews are over, so it's well worth while having a chat with her in a very general way about the company. You can also check how to pronounce the interviewer's name if there is any doubt.

6   Here are a few tips that will gain you ticks and help ensure you are not rejected in the first 90 seconds: Your dress. How you enter the room. Thanking the secretary who shows you into the room. Using the interviewer's name. Showing yourself to be as much at ease as you can—this will come only with interview practice.

7   Why are you leaving your job? What interests you in this job? What are your future career plans? You live at so and so—are you willing to move nearer the company? How would you cope with this crisis situation? What salary are you looking for?
   Then for the second part of the question, compare your answers with the advice given in the chapter.

8   Compare your answer with the list of job successes in the personal information forms you completed in Chapter 6.

9   Be careful how you answer—you can price yourself out of a job by asking too little as well as too much. If you have done your homework properly you will know roughly what the job should pay and how this relates to what you want.
   If you don't know what to say, ask the interviewer what the company has in mind as a guide and answer

accordingly. If the subject isn't raised, don't raise it yourself at this first interview.

10   Immediately the interview is over, make a critical self-examination of your performance at the interview—note down the questions you were asked and the answers you wish you had given. Add the new questions to your list—they will surely come up again.

Chapter 17: The Final Interview

1   Your aim now is the job—to get to the top of the short-list. In the earlier interviews your aim was to stay on the short-list.

2   Although you will continue to sell yourself, you will spend more time asking questions about the job and the part you will play, because this is the last opportunity you will have to ensure you want the job if it is offered to you.

3   The third list consists of the questions you want to ask yourself about your *impressions* of the company and the people you have met.

4   Can I work with this man (or woman)? Are we on the same wavelength? Have we any common interests? Will there be a personality clash? Has he a sense of humour? Is there a good atmosphere in the company? Shall I be free to make decisions?

5   The principal items are: The advertisement. Your letter of application. A copy of your CV. The company information form. Your notes made after the previous interviews. The lists, A, B and C, comprising the questions you expect to be asked, the questions you want to ask and questions about your impression of the company.

6   Secretarial and personal assistant.

7   How many interviewers, their names and job titles. You

may have been given this information in the letter inviting you to the interview. Otherwise ask the secretary or receptionist.

8 To see whether your replies are consistent or whether you have forgotten what you said if you had 'bent the truth' in the previous interview.

9 The person to whom you will be directly responsible (assuming he or she is present) to determine whether there is a rapport between you.

10 First make your notes on the interview, then continue your job-getting campaign unabated until you are made an offer and have accepted.

Index